The Narcissist Notebook

A Collection of Toxic Tales

Edited by Lindzi Mayann

13/11/2020

Poems, stories, thoughts and advice from a collection of real people. A variety of experiences and situations have been penned with the mission of raising awareness and providing support for all.

The Narcissist Notebook

Contents

Welcome to

The Narcissist Notebook

Or rather, BE WARNED!
The stories in this book are shocking, crazy, bizarre, unsettling and everything in between!

So, a huge THANK YOU for purchasing your copy, just in case you decide to put it back down now.
And, of course, a shout out to those brave, broken, nuts and oh-so-over-it devils that shared their experiences and made this collection a reality.

You should know the main idea is to RAISE AWARENESS and INSPIRE:

We want to raise awareness that toxic relationships can be really damaging, that they- unfortunately- happen all the time and all around us.

We are also donating our proceeds to charity.

We want to inspire others to feel strong, let go of shame, regret and bitterness, move on, relate and understand, heal and feel every bit of positivity in between.

These are true stories, shared by real people and written in their own words (very lightly edited by me- Lindzi Mayann).

Of course, there is always another side to a story- so if you have something to say, get in touch and share away. A second edition is already anticipated.

Also, for those who feel this isn't a fair approach- well, the world isn't a fair place for a start.

And when we say we want to inspire- that does include those who are doing the damage; seek help!

Find support and break the cycle.

There is no 'name and shame' about this. I have always used a pen to exercise my demons.

I felt honoured to be reading each one of these submissions and was pleased to hear feedback that writing it all down helped some of these people too.

It was, of course, a triggering experience for many as well who found writing this content painful and difficult.

So please, think carefully about how any feedback is worded.

I am sure some who took part in this unusual opportunity saw it as a chance to get their own back.
Well, what can I say?
My Jodie Trilogy cleverly dissects my ex. It was better than slashing his tyres (he didn't drive anyway, ha).
BUT in my eyes, the best revenge is success, moving on, being the same old fantastic person you always were.

I hope being a part of this book- whether that be contributing or reading the stories- helps someone with this. So, enjoy the ride.

I'll begin by explaining a few terms.

Terms

A 'narcissist':

They have an 'inflated' sense of their own importance- this won't exactly jump out at you (in hindsight it will of course!) Narcissists are clever and you'll fall for how amazing they are- because they create the illusion of being this 'special' person.

Conversations will focus on their achievements, their talents, skills and differences (all things which set them apart from anything 'standard').

At first they might include you in this 'special' category (love bombing) however this won't last *or* could co-exist alongside put downs and subtle (or not so subtle) insults.
A narcissist may see your beauty, success or popularity as an extension of their own achievements. They may present you to others with high regard and 'show you off' like a trophy.

They have a 'deep need' for excessive attention.
They may seem to just generate this admiration- because they'll surround themselves with people who serve this purpose. And they'll be interested in actually looking good. Thanks to their 'inflated' sense of self importance they'll have already won many people over with boasts and claims- exaggerated or otherwise (lies).
This trait includes what I refer to as needing an 'ego rub'.

Basically fishing for compliments, dangling carrots to encourage you to chase them or pushing and pulling (playing hot and cold) with their affection- again to get you running and begging.

It's worth mentioning a narcissist, despite their over-bearing confidence, tends to have very low self-esteem. You may or may not recognise this. If you realise their secret vulnerability it can add to their hold over you. (You might feel sorry for them/ be drawn to help them. You'll be in love with their potential. Empaths will experience this in particular.)

The narcissist *needs* admiration the same way a car needs energy to run. They will enjoy being around those who worship them and spend time creating a facade of being of the highest beauty, success and/ or intelligence.

A narcissist may 'use' their appearance and/ or body in garnering attention from the opposite sex.
They might also use all of the above to climb a career ladder and/ or in social status.

Troubled relationships. This can materialise within any area of their life- and possibly all.
This doesn't mean they don't have relationships or can't maintain relationships/ friendships. But since a narcissist is completely selfish (and doesn't realise it at all) they will surround themselves with people who meet their needs.

You could have 'friendships' with narcissists and chances are they use you for something. It could be physical (alcohol, money, a place to hang out), you might feed their ego or they could see your intelligence/ looks/ personality as something of a benefit to their own image.

Nothing about any past failed relationship will be their fault. They might sweet talk you with learned balance (they can be very smart and perceptive) and may say, I know this was my fault or I know I did wrong here.

But ultimately, anything from a job loss to a breakdown with a lover is someone else's fault because of 'this' or 'that'.

Lack of empathy for others.

This isn't a case of 'not caring'- a narcissist *can't* care. They won't lose sleep over their actions because they just aren't mulling things over the way a regular person might.

A narcissist *will* show they care. If they lose control, you'll experience them 'caring'. They'll 'care' if their image might become tarnished. They will show they 'care' if you make a decision that doesn't benefit them.

Ultimately they'll say whatever to win you over. And they won't change- because they don't 'suffer' from hindsight.

Since they lack this capacity for empathy a narcissist won't learn from their mistakes and so history will seem to repeat itself.

If you have been- or suspect that you are- in a relationship with a narcissist you will likely have experienced the following tactics.

Gas-lighting: This refers to making a person question their memories and reality of a situation in order to bend/ alter the truth. A narcissist will deny things (such as cheating) even in the face of evidence- even if you saw something with your own eyes! They'll use things against you, switch the focus and change the argument until you're spinning and questioning yourself. Did it actually even happen that way? Are you going crazy? Suddenly it's all your fault.

Love bombing: This is how the narcissist wins you over. They will shower you with overwhelming affection. The purpose is to gain control and ultimately manipulate you. It can be extra powerful since you already think *they* are so amazing- the fact they feel this way about you is just WOW!

Narcissistic personality disorder is a mental condition and can only be officially diagnosed by a qualified professional.

In my experience it is possible for people to be 'narcissistic' and have strong traits (as described above). And these characteristics may be stronger or more noticeable during times of mental stress.

A true narcissist cannot be cured, their tendencies will always be there, but therapy can help.

'Fuck Boy'- this means a player, ladies man, known to get about with the females and a flirt. A fuck boy may have narcissistic qualities such as arrogance, selfishness, a big ego etc.

Empath- somebody who has great empathy. Empathy is more than feeling sorry for someone (sympathy) it means really 'feeling' the pain, upset, turmoil, happiness of another. It can be a draining 'super power' since an empath naturally tunes in and takes on the energy be it good or bad.

Feeling trapped with a narcissistic lover/ person in your life? At the back of this book you can find a list of help lines and support plus advice gathered from real people who want to help you!

A Brief History of my Experience with Narcs

By Lindzi Mayann

For as long as I can remember I have been an absolute sucker for a bad boy.

If he ain't trouble (hopefully with a capital T) then he just ain't turning me on. And I've long given up on deciding what came first- the attraction to red flags OR the ability to single these fuckers out.

What I do know by now, and accept, is my vagina is an amoral, traitorous little bitch. I'm blaming her like she flares up with desire the moment I spot one of these guys.
No. It's all in the eye contact actually. A chemical surge. A *feeling*. But they're definitely related since it's only when I feel this way I'll even contemplate having sex.
Lucky me. Although they are usually hot at least.

So, if that 'spark' happens I can absolutely guarantee the object of my desire is a rebel. And possibly, likely, gunna be bad news for my mental state.
Do I care? Hell no. Wave those red flags!
It's a feeling like no other. A thrill, powerful excitement. And something that can't be faked- it usually turns out to be the only genuine thing in the whole relationship!

Did I mention the guy always turns out to be a dick head?

Luckily, but unfortunately for my sex life, the kind of man that catches my eye in this way is few and far between.

I know for certain- and I'm rather proud- that I have a one hundred per cent hit rate at falling for guys with narcissistic tendencies. I specialise in arrogance, selfishness, opinionated, good-looking, materialistic, egotistical, unique, rule-breakers and cocky men.

I can't help it! It's an uncontrollable attraction. And these guys don't even *look* the same- they just make me *feel* the same crazy, nauseous, spellbound way.
Twenty years of it and counting!

Teen Years
I recently found a box of poetry I'd written aged nine to sixteen.
The later stuff was so full of love, then heartbreak and torment- it reminded me of a number of relationships- four undoubtedly 'bad boys'- two of which were *incredibly* toxic, two of which were rocky and crazy but I still adore the guys and speak to them both.

This attraction to 'wrong uns' must have initially put me off and I found myself in a very secure and settled relationship for three years which I ended in my very early twenties.

Twenties
My 20's introduced me to the guy my dad warned me about.

You can read a version of this relationship in my book, Pub Life. As I mentioned before I have always used words as a tool to release my emotions and since he made me feel like shit, I thought I'd return the favour and use him as a villain for my story.

Particularly since he laughed at my ambitions to become an author in the first place.

Remember, success speaks volumes.

And despite it being a horrible thing to go through- I was always kind of thankful for the experience. It made me much quicker to cut the crap in relationships in future.

Something I needed in my twenties (and thirties so far).

Thirties

Again, perhaps traumatised by the string of fuck-boys and narcs encountered in my twenties, I had a pretty settled two year relationship as I entered my thirties.

And when this was over, returned to my single life thinking I had it all sorted.

Then I got my mind fucked sideways by a guy who is actually every narcissist description I have read since. Perhaps it was worse because I thought I had it sussed.

I met him and was playing the game- I didn't want anything serious and neither did he. Or did he? He was very full on. He'd tell me he wanted us to have babies, that they'd be so beautiful. We would rule the world. He called me perfect, I should have known then- but I honestly was mesmerised by him. I'd known of him for years, only as a very distant person and always thought he was the fittest thing to walk this planet.

And now here he was, all the time, telling me how hot and amazing I am!

I know I can hold my own in the interesting person department. He could match me and more. I loved that about him- finally someone with substance and varied stories to tell. We got along like we had known each forever. And I fancied the actual pants off him.

He tapped into me and presented me with a guy I couldn't have dreamt up better myself. He was 'intellectual', he enjoyed 'deep' conversation, told me how 'the same' we were because both of us dared to be different. And we did have lots in common- a love for partying and music!

I didn't know then how much of it was a show.

He was fairly newly single and out of a long-term relationship. He would tell me he wasn't cut out for a relationship, he was misunderstood and all that. I am happy single so I thought what we had was a good set up.

He was lively and 'over the top' but I've always been hyper and I loved being around him.

After a few weeks he just stopped turning up. He stopped following through with promises to visit me. For weeks I'd see him around a lot, things would be like how they always had been, we'd message and then, well, nothing. At first it was put down to getting drunk, mates distracting him, whatever.

Then one night we were in the smoking shelter and being our usual selves when he said,

"You're obsessed with me, aren't you? I'm glad, that's how I wanted to get you."

I'll never forget the look in his eye.

I'd already resolved I would never be *that* girl. This guy was 'dripping in pussy' literally. Everywhere he goes he turns heads. He loved female attention. He had a certain few who were obsessed over him and I was never going to be one of those.

But not only did I feel absolutely fucking crazy by this point, it also confirmed what I already suspected; he *was* getting a kick out of toying with me, he *was* doing it on purpose.

It was like an experiment gone wrong.

It hurt more because I'd really thought we were friends. We were so alike and had so much fun, we bounced off each other. It didn't make sense to prefer messing with my head. But there was the truth.

He'd got me exactly where he wanted me and I *still* couldn't cut him off completely even with his words ringing in my mind. You're obsessed. I'm glad. Wanted to.

We kept bumping into each other, we'd flirt, chat on text, he'd lead me on and leave me hanging. I couldn't help myself from wanting him and he acted like he still wanted me too.

I felt like I was watching it all unfold as though I was a bystander screaming, *stop! STOP!-* but I was helpless to stop. He had taken over my mind. I felt out of control for those few weeks.

I had no idea I was under the spell of a narcissist- even though he reminded me so much of some of the guys I have fell for in the past. Ironically I took this as a good sign- perhaps he was my perfect match since he reminded me of them.

Actually it was just 'my type' kicking in again. Another dick head.

In hindsight I discovered he had fed me a combination of lies and exaggerations perfectly matched with me- who I am as a person and the kind of people I like.

He was a chameleon, and a perceptive one at that. So smart I almost respect his calculating!

He presented me with an image of exactly what I would have wanted from a guy. He'd already convinced me to see him in the first place (I just knew he would be bad news!) Then he love bombed me, used me for his needs and dropped me when the next best thing came along.

He finally admitted to me one night that he had been *a bit distant* because he'd got a new girlfriend (I had suspected something and it all added up) I actually felt relieved in a weird way, at least something I'd been thinking was correct. I replied that he only had to tell me. He said that was why he was telling me now.

If I'd truly understood what had gone on I would have said, no you're telling me now because you don't need me anymore.

That part was over in a matter of a few months but it left me reeling. He carried on toying with me and I carried on letting him.

I had to remind myself over and over that the guy I fell for isn't even *him*. I fell for, then broke my heart over, a guy that doesn't even exist!!! He isn't the same guy in front of everyone.

Who knows what the real version is, maybe not even he knows nowadays.

I knew about narcissism by my late twenties- recognised I'd been through it even, but I didn't realise when I was going through it again. And not for a long time after either.

Reading about narcissism in more detail was a real shock when I related to every single description and explanation. It confirmed what I already knew- I'd been duped. And had a lucky escape by all accounts since his attentions turned elsewhere!

It was a short and intense encounter. I've always been an open and free-spirit but it made me feel wary about how much I must give away without realising. I questioned my own judgement for a while until I considered I knew from the start I was making a bad decision.

This Summer, following more bad decisions, I shared a meme saying something along the lines of,

'Who was out there happily looking for the one but found themselves with a degree in psychology specialising in narcissistic personality disorder?'

It had really made me laugh since by this point I had realised I have a natural talent for attracting narc-type men.
And the response got this book going. So how could I not be thankful for that?

The whole experience with him forced me to take a proper look at myself and ask just exactly what I wanted- for me. It pushed me forward, egged me on to keep chasing my dreams. It all ultimately motivated me to do better and keep moving.
Never mind being a further education in love- or lust rather.
Nothing wrong with refresher training since fuck boys got upgraded to fucking psychos.

I am still single and still loving it- most of the time. I adore a red flag, I have no desire to 'settle' down, and my experiences haven't put me off.

I have discovered the extreme sport of 'fishing for narcs' and feel more prepared than ever.

There are probably reasons why I am spellbound by rejection and competing with an unsatisfiable ego. I just know I enjoy being kept on my toes much more than I relish in routine.

I may just be addicted to the thrill or in love with lust, rather than love itself. I'm probably a psychologist's wet-dream. All I know for sure is, I kinda like the challenge.

So, wish me luck for the future! I am beyond help but I hope you guys take some meaningful inspiration from our stories.

Barber's Twist

By Jade

Circa 2008, I was eighteen and working at a bar in Wigan. One of my duties was to go down King Street and hand out fliers for free drinks to try and get a bit of custom.

It was mad busy but I couldn't help but notice this gorgeous looking guy with an enviable tan, long, brown, curly hair with a rugby player build and an amazing smile. I had the perfect excuse to approach him.

My hand stretched out, I said, "Free drink with this flier at *insert bar name here*."

To which he responded, '*I'll come, but only if you write your number on the back.*' ...smooth.

He took the flier and walked away.
Later that night I was on my break, having a fag with a friend outside when I spotted that beaming smile walking toward me.

"You didn't write your number on here!" He waved the flier in my face.

I took my phone out of my pocket and said, "If you want it that bad, then here," and passed him my phone. "My name's Jade."

He took my number down and buzzed my phone, "Mine's Joel," He said.

He proceeded to walk inside the bar and I carried on with the hustle and bustle of a busy bar on a Friday night and went home.

I didn't hear anything from him.

A few days passed and I get a text;

'Hey! It's Joel from Wigan. Are you working again this weekend?'

My stomach flipped.

'I'm working on Friday but off Saturday and Sunday. Why? Are you out?'

'No, but I was wondering if I could take you out?'

Long story short, we arranged a date and time and enjoyed each other's company and became casual.

A few months passed and, typical woman, I asked the question, 'where are we?'. Turned out he just wanted to keep things casual which, in hindsight, should've been a red flag but I had developed feelings for him at this point so I continued to be the cat to his mouse for a while.

It was disheartening to say the least. He kept telling me that he just 'wasn't ready for a relationship', yet we still did everything that a couple would do. It was confusing. My first and only relationship prior to Joel was with a guy a few years my senior who had his head screwed on and knew what he wanted. So, I didn't have much to go off experience-wise and I ended up thinking this was normal for guys my own age.

Anyway, I had no choice but to go with the flow.

It was coming up to Halloween. I had been invited to my friend's party at her halls of residence at Manchester Uni and she asked me to bring Joel along so that she could meet him. I saw him later that day and I asked if he would like to be my plus one, to which he responded, "Only if you'll be my girlfriend?"

YES! We were officially official.

On the night of the Halloween party, we had pre-drinks at my friend's dorm and hit the clubs of Manchester.
We bar-hopped for a few hours, everyone was getting along well, or so I thought. Joel cornered me and asked if we could ditch my friends and go stay at his dad's who lived nearby. I couldn't 'ditch' my friends, that's not the person I am. I lied and told them that Joel wasn't feeling too good and that we were going home.

This soon came to be a regular occurrence when mixing Joel and my friends and eventually, I came to end up with no friends left.

Joel's dad was a middle-eastern man who moved to the UK in the 80's and pursued a career as a chef.
Joel later followed in his dad's footsteps and became a chef himself, great for me! But Joel had warned me, prior to meeting his dad, that his views are much different to ours.
I seemed to pass the dad test, until one night I was over at Joel's mum's house and his dad called him. Joel was giving it the old 'I know, yeah, ok, I know' and then I heard his dad say, 'DO NOT TELL HER YOU LOVE HER!'.
Welp. I didn't question it.
Tip. Of. The. Iceberg. Get the popcorn ready lads n gals. This is where shit starts to go down, FAST.

Things seemed to go smoothly for a year or so, until I lost my job. I was a student at college and along with Jobseekers Allowance, I wasn't particularly bothered about a job as my studies would lead me to employment anyway.

But my unemployment didn't sit well with Joel and he said that he wanted a 'break' until I got another job.

At the time, unemployment was rife so I was challenged to get a job in such a climate just to get my boyfriend to want to be with me again! I managed, but as a result of the stress of everything, had my first taste of depression with anxiety and ended up being a bad employee. Turning up late from struggling to sleep the night before, calling in sick because my work days didn't coincide with his, being caught on my phone too much because I was texting him to let him know I wasn't near any male colleagues, as per his request.

When he came to pick me up to take me on dates or just if he wanted to come and visit me, he started to ask me for petrol money. Seriously. Just because he drove 15 minutes to see me.

I told my family about this as I wasn't clued up on petrol costs and whatnot as I didn't drive, but apparently this wasn't normal. Fair enough if he asked me to chip in for a long journey say if we were going on a trip, but not just a boyfriend visiting his girlfriend.

I should have added this at the beginning but I can't put things in to an exact timeline anymore. Things seem to stick in my mind as 'bad shit my ex did' rather than 'when my ex did this bad thing'. But now I'll take you to my 21st birthday...

We had arranged, just he and I and his friends, to meet at whatever time in whatever pub in Wigan for my birthday celebrations.

I got to said pub at said time and he wasn't there. Tried calling and texting, no response. About an hour had passed, I got a text saying, '*me and Craig are just finishing up on a quest on World of Warcraft then we'll be there*'.

Shortly after, an old, male, high school friend came in to the pub and noticed me sat by myself wearing my 21st birthday badge and he asked what was going on.

I filled him in and he bought me a shot of tequila to 'celebrate', but it was really a pity shot.

JUST as I was having the shot, Joel walked in to the pub with his friend Craig and his other friend Fiona. I always liked Craig but we'll get back to Fiona.

Joel put a friendly face on and said, "Do you want to come for a cig?"

So I obliged and went out the rear entrance of the pub which led in to a quiet, dimly lit alley and he immediately slapped me across the face for accepting the shot from my high school friend.

That should have been an instant dismissal but I just went in to a sort of shock-like state and continued on with my birthday 'celebrations'.

Side note - World Of Warcraft was a huge issue in the relationship. I don't mind blokes playing video games. I enjoy them myself occasionally, it's not a problem, but Joel had an actual addiction. It was obsessive too and he actually seemed to have withdrawals if he didn't play for a couple of days.

Whenever I would be at his house, 90% of the time I would be sat on his bed staring at the back of his head and it would really hurt because I was there to spend time with him, not be ignored.

One particular New Year's Eve, we said we weren't bothered about doing anything as with Wigan tradition, Boxing Day is the big night out, which we did.

So we agreed we were spending time with our respective families. After all, I had no mates to do anything with because he'd made me unintentionally force them away.

So in the evening I noticed that he was unusually quiet. I text to ask if he was ok, no response.
Midnight rolled around, I wished him a happy new year, no response. 1am, getting slightly worried, I called him, no answer. I called him again, a female voice said '*hello*' and let out a sly little snigger.
I cried all night, I didn't sleep. I was crushed.

The day after, he got in touch via text to brand me a 'psycho' for texting and ringing 'too much' and broke up with me.

Weeks passed and he decided he wanted to meet up for a 'talk'.
I met him in a pub in Wigan and I asked him why he broke up with me.
'Because I wanted to smash some poon,' he said.

It felt like a stab in the fucking guts. Arsehole. But guess what? He concluded that he wanted to get back together and I was thrilled. I was in love with him. Despite everything.
Looking back, I think about how childish that statement and the word 'poon' is.
It still isn't nice to think about that moment but I have to admit, he was acting like a fifteen year old.
Things were ok at best.

He did come out with the odd little put-down such as, 'I've shagged better looking girls than you,' and one time I met him on my lunch at college and I was wearing my college tunic and a mid-length skirt with tights and he said I was dressed like a slut and accused me of cheating because there was a ladder in my tights.

In actual fact I sustained said ladder with a hairbrush in the college hair salon.

He belittled me to the point where I became a shell of my former self.

Jade wasn't there anymore.

He also liked to minimise my achievements. I passed my college course with flying colours and I was buzzing.

Why wouldn't I be?

His response was, "It's only hairdressing. Everyone knows hairdressers are thick."

I got full marks on the science and chemistry side of the exam, science has always been my strong subject. How's that for 'thick'?

I still went on to do barbering too.

We went away to Dublin. It was for my 22nd birthday, I think. We had a really good night, met some lovely people and headed back to the hotel.

Joel was a bit worse for wear and I attempted to give him some ibuprofen and a glass of water before bed so that he wouldn't wake up as rough in the morning, you know, because I care like that.

He slapped the glass from my hand, grabbed my wrist and shoved me back in to the wall and said, "You don't get to tell me what to do!"

I didn't retaliate and I pretty much let it slide due to the fact he was drunk.

Now I realise, maybe he didn't like me having such a good time and needed to knock me down and spoil it for me.

It was recently my 30th birthday and due to Covid, it got cancelled. In a way I was relieved because of Joel spoiling every one of my birthdays and my anxiety just kept telling me something else would spoil my 30th if it had gone ahead.

When it came to his birthday, though, things were different. He liked to smoke weed, so he wanted to go to Amsterdam. I was happy to go but I'm not one for recreational drugs which he would use as some sort of deterrent to try and put me off going.

He told me near the time of booking, "I just want it to be a lads' holiday, so it's just going to be me and Craig."

I was fine with that, didn't bother me in the slightest but he kept insisting it was just him and Craig which I thought was odd.

A few days later, we were at his dad's with his sister, Gabriella and we were sat in the living room. Gabriella was on the phone to their dad's girlfriend and she excitedly blurted out, "Oh! I nearly forgot to tell you, me, Joel and Craig are going to Amsterdam!"

I looked at Joel in disbelief. Why wouldn't he tell me his sister was going with them? It's his sister! I wouldn't have been arsed, but why keep it a secret? I didn't get it. I never mentioned anything. He just said it was last minute.

I think it was the same year, we went for his birthday meal with his family and Gabriella had invited her friend Nat. Come to think of it, it must have been Gabriella's birthday.

Nat and Joel sat opposite, I was sat on Joel's left.

Nat and Joel blatantly flirted with each other for the entirety of the meal, to the point where they were even fucking feeding each other.

I left before everyone had even finished their food, said I felt sick, which I did.

Still never mentioned anything to him though for fear of causing an argument.

Every time I would mention anything that I wasn't happy about, he gas lighted me and would make me feel as though it was my fault and tell me I was 'pushing him away', and then I would apologise for something he did.

Mind fuck.

Another situation has just come to mind which may be quite funny to you, reader, but it still affects me to this day. I (now) see myself as quite attractive, albeit chunky from all the lockdown binging, haha. But it's only weight. So yeah, I believe I am pretty. We were at Gabriella's halls of residence in Leeds for New Year's Eve.

The night was fine, good fun. Anyhow, everyone had gone to bed and myself and Joel were having sex. I was on top and he said 'you look like a monkey when you're having sex'.

After that, and even now, I have to either cover my face with a pillow or face away from my husband. And when I'm on top I lie on him so that he can't see my face. Fortunately my husband understands but wishes that I would let him look at me.

As I mentioned earlier, he liked to smoke weed. Like, really liked it. It was a weekly occurrence. I tried to ask him if he would mind not getting stoned when I was there because I wanted to spend time with him when he was compos mentis. He disagreed and basically told me to like it or lump it.

So one night he was out in his garden having a spliff and I thought to myself, 'well if you can't beat them, join them'.

I asked him if I could have a bit and he obliged.

About thirty minutes later, I felt a strange sensation in my chest, like a wave of ice. My heart was pounding. I can't even begin to describe the overwhelming amount of fear that was taking hold of me.

I screamed to him to call for an ambulance which he did.

I thought my heart was going to explode.

The paramedics came, I told them the truth, they took me in to hospital. It was diagnosed as a panic attack.

For months later, they kept happening and I refused to believe they were panic attacks, I thought I had a heart problem.

My family were sick to the back teeth of my weekly trips to the GP. I was in a bad mental state. All the events after this were a blur.

I remember him always wanting the best of everything, best car, best motorbike, best PC. He always shot me down for not having brand name clothes, I don't care about brand names. Anyhow, I was no exception in coming under that category. What was I the best at though? What made me the best? My eagerness to please and being complacent and accept all of his shit? I will never know.

Suddenly, I was no longer the best and he asked for a break. AGAIN.

This time the best was a burlesque dancer. I don't know where the fuck they met or even her name. All he told me was that she was a burlesque dancer and she was amazing in bed. Nice.

After a short while, probably when he realised she wouldn't take any of his shit, he came running back to me, the mug.

We went to Download festival a couple of times.

One time we went just the two of us, another time we went with Craig, Joel's other friend Fiona and her friends, 'Crunchy' and Andy. I loved Crunchy, he was fucking funny, but always off his tits.

I don't think I ever encountered him sober. He was like Fun Bobby from Friends. Craig was lovely too, a gentle giant. 6ft 10" at least. He was so timid and shy.

But anyway, Fiona, Crunchy and Andy were all in to drugs. Fiona was actually a drugs counsellor. Hello?! Defeating the object much?

Crunchy was too spaced out to care much about anything, but Fiona and Andy spent the whole time forcing Craig to take this or that, I could see he didn't want to so I confronted them which led to Joel kicking off at me for kicking off at them, and they all ditched me.

Left me on my own at a huge music festival with hundreds of thousands of people with no fucking phone.

Joel was studying Culinary Arts at college throughout our relationship. It had come to the point where he was considering going to university. Because I am the kind of person that wants the best for everybody, I encouraged him to go.

Everything he did that was career related, I supported him, I was his biggest cheerleader.

Eventually, he decided on Buxton University as it was the best for Culinary Arts, he got in. I was delighted for him and I was bursting with pride.

Love made me blind to the fact that he saw Uni as an opportunity to 'smash some poon' and get hammered every night.

Once again, he dumped me. Only this time, I had no hope we would get back together because he had a new life now, so I got back in touch with a few old friends.

One being a married man called Chris, who was utterly and completely my best friend. He was my shining star that picked me up from rock bottom.

We hung out all the time with his wife, Amy and his brother, Kian. We loved watching the rugby together and going out for breakfasts.

It was everything I needed at that time and I finally felt like a part of something again. I was involved in situations, I was asked for my opinions, I was valued in a friendship.

It was good. Jade was coming back.

I remember Kian once referring to me as a 'hot, sane chick' which was a far cry from what I was made to believe I really was!

A few weeks or so went by and I had a text from Joel. He invited me to come to Buxton as a 'friend'. I was more than happy to go, being a friend was better than nothing. Whilst we were there, there was another girl, I can't remember her name, but she was a little too touchy-feely with him.

I kept my mouth shut, I was Joel's friend. Well, until later that night, Joel asked me to be his girlfriend again. I accepted.

Once I returned home, I lived my life as normal. I saw my friends too, but because Joel was so far away, it was easier to lie and live a double life of sorts.

I still went to see him a couple of times a month, but when I was home, I did what I wanted to do. I never really felt any guilt over it. I wasn't doing anything that society would deem as wrong. I didn't realise at the time but this was me becoming a stronger person.

Each week, I could feel myself becoming more and more desensitised to Joel's bullshit. It was bliss.

I think he noticed as he started to tell me things like, 'I don't want to lose you' and ask, 'are we ok?'.

I assured him we were fine. Deep down, his uncertainty was giving me a bit of a thrill.

I will admit I was no angel throughout the relationship.

I got drunk a few times and that annoyed him, but I never belittled him or said anything hurtful to him. Nor did I act out in such a way that warranted anything he ever did or said to me. But knowing he was questioning my feelings for him gave me a little buzz.

Around this time, he admitted that he had insecurities about his appearance as he was going bald. He was around twenty-two at the time. I get that it's a young age to be losing your hair and I can understand how it would make him insecure.

I bought him several bottles of Alpecin shampoo, around £18 a pop. He took petrol money from me for fuck all, but never offered to reimburse me for the shampoo. Petty of me to bring this up, I know, but I never asked for the money back, it just would've been nice if he offered to pay me back for it.

It was summer. Joel was due home from Uni for summer break. I was still hanging out with Chris and his wife and brother but I just notched the sneakiness level up a little. Chris told me that Kian had mentioned that he fancied me and I thought he was really fit too. He was nice to me, he complemented me, went out of his way for me. A gentleman.

I don't condone cheating so nothing like that ever happened but it felt nice to be wanted.

One night I was at Joel's. His mum told me that she managed to arrange a boat trip holiday around the Greek islands for three weeks. Joel, Gabriella and his mum and step-dad. Turned out there was no signal wherever they were and Joel was radio silent for the entire three weeks. IT WAS AMAZING!

It felt as though I was broken free from the shackles. I loved it. I knew what I needed to do.

Joel calls me from the airport to say he'd just landed back at Manchester.

I was nonchalant.

He noticed something wasn't right and asked what was wrong.

I just blurted out, "I don't want to be with you anymore, it's over, I don't want this anymore, don't contact me again."

I know it's pretty mean to dump someone over the phone but fuck it, after all he did to me, he kinda deserved it.

I had text after text after text, I ignored and ignored and ignored.

It got to a point where it was actual harassment.

I gave in and responded. He wanted to talk. I agreed, just to get him to leave me the fuck alone.

He met me at my house.

He asked me if we could have sex 'one last time'.

I said, 'so if I do this with you, will you leave me alone?' He nodded. Ok.

I told him that I was literally just going to lie there because I didn't want to do it, that was fine according to him. I lay down, pants off. He puts his D inside my V and bursts in to tears, thrusts once and cums.

If that isn't the most beautiful bit of karma then I don't know what is!

Afterwards, he continued with the texts and calls. I was at my mum's house with her. My phone was buzzing, I answered, '*please stop calling and texting, I have told you so many fucking times that I don't want to be with you anymore!!*'

And hung up.

Seconds later, I got a text, 'I want to eradicate you from my life'.

My mum and I absolutely pissed ourselves laughing, it was fucking hilarious.

"Eradicate!!!" I said with what little breath I had between the belly laughs.

And that was that.

He never contacted me again. The break up was on my terms, the only time it was on my terms and it stuck. Thank fuck for that, I was free.

Around eighteen months later, I actually hadn't had a sexual partner for about sixteen of those months. I had hooked up with Kian for a brief period but we always had protected sex.

So I was in a pub with a mate and we went to the loo. We walked in to the toilets and there were a couple of those people who offer STI screenings for you to do yourself so I thought there's no harm in doing one! A few days later, I get a phone call;

"Hello, is that Miss *surname*?"

"Yes, speaking."

"This is Linda from St. Helen's sexual health service. You did a screening recently and I'm just calling you to inform you that you have tested positive for Chlamydia. You need to attend St. Helens GUM clinic at the hospital for treatment."

Well, shit. It was obviously passed on to me by Joel, but when?!

I didn't know how long I had it. I definitely had it for longer than eighteen months but how much longer??

I spent a lot of time afterwards believing that I'm probably infertile. I had two miscarriages and that's what I thought was happening. I thought I couldn't have kids because of that prick.

I still, also, suffer with anxiety because of him. It's engrained in to me now. I have had help and I am better but he was the root cause of it.

Many, many moons later, in the present day, I am married to the kindest man I have ever known. I appreciate how lucky I am to have him every single day.

He is my rock, my world and the best daddy to our two amazing little boys. I am truly happy.

Yes we have had ups and downs but nothing malicious. We've never been mean to one another, shit happens and that's a marriage, but by god, I know I would do anything for the three of them and my husband would do anything for the three of us.

I got my happily ever after.

Groundhog Day

By Gary Clarke

"Oi you lazy bitch, get off the fuckin' sofa.
I've been work all day and this is your soap opera."

"Who the fuck you speaking to? This is my house too!"
"Who pays the rent bitch? Me, not fuckin' you!"

"But I do all the cleaning, even make your tea."
"So where the fuck is it then? What you cooked for me?"

"Well I've got to peel some spuds and wash a couple of pans."
Right around her fucking neck I want to put my hands.

Instead, I throw my phone and it bounces off the wall.
Then the narcky bitch shouts, *"What you do that for?"*

I'm mumbling, my mind goes off another fucking way.
"What was that you said? What you fucking say?"

I'm not going to help myself, my hands are around her throat.
I'm screaming, "Shut the fuck up bitch," she starts to fuckin' choke.

She's turning blue on me, I have to stop and think.
'Should I fuckin kill this bitch, or let her turn back pink?'

I release my grip and then she starts to come around.
I just fucking leave her there, gasping on the ground.

This volatile relationship will get one of us killed.
The way she fucking looks at me, I think she should be thrilled.

I then turn and leave and head towards the bars,
I'm now so fucking angry and my head is up my arse.

Later I arrive home pissed. To me she's fucking dead.
Twenty minutes later and we're fucking in our bed.

See how I said 'ours' and not just fuckin' 'mine'?
Our so called relationship is falling in decline.

Should we have a chat about it, or should I walk away?
Because maybe this is just my fucking ground hog day.

The Narcissistic Other

By Asante Mist

Teenage Love…..

So here goes. It started when I was 16, young and dumb, but I just knew he was everything to me.

At that age people always say, 'oh its young love you'll grow out of it,' and so on. But for me, I knew he was the one. I wanted to spend my life with him and being the over confident person I am, I made him very aware lol.

I'd always tell him how I was going to have his babies and we would grow old together. At 16, I can be and it probably was a bit full on, but fuck it, that's just me.

Then the break up happened and I was a mess. He wanted to go live his life and be a lad which to some degree, I understood. We was young and we had our whole lives to live and I just knew this was the end. It was just time to go experience life.

Over the years…..

Of course then over the years I'd been in multiple relationships, but none that truly felt like they was enough. I just couldn't scratch that itch and feel the feeling I felt like with him. So, obviously, I did what we all do and social media searched my way onto his page. And then back into his life.

Then it seemed to be a regular thing, a relationship didn't work because I'd constantly think about him. To the point I'd date people so similar it was ridiculous (also sad and slightly obsessive I know) and then I'd end up contacting him. We ended up right back to the start every time. Our banter never changed, the easy flow of each other's company. It was just perfect but we never would fully commit to each other because we had our own things going on. Plus my family hated him and so on. So we called it a day.

Fast forward a few more years.......

He's now got a child....

I am super happy for him and we have rekindled again. Clearly can't leave each other alone but that was a given.

Now the *real* problems start.

The mother of his child is crazy. They are no longer together just to be clear. But I do not know what to do! She demands to know where he is or what he's doing and if it isn't going her way then she makes it very difficult for him to see his child.

I'm at my wits end. We must keep our relationship a secret or he loses out.

We are at a place where he's basically stuck between a rock and a hard place and I just do not know what to do.

I love him and always will, but we both know she has full control. He can't make plans, she has him running around like an idiot because if he doesn't the result will always be the same. No access to his child.

It's now at the point her narcissistic ways are affecting my life and I'm torn. Do I walk away from the man of my dreams after I have waited so long, or do I ride it out?

Advice needed........

Predator Wears Prada

By Lizzie Moore

Like most young women it's fair to say that I have dated my fair share of dickheads. Most girls I admired seemed to have a superpower when it came to the opposite sex, whether it be batting ridiculously long eyelashes or seductively flicking glossy fabulous tresses- of which I had neither.

My particular skill, or curse, was attracting every fuckwit within a five mile radius.

When I was younger and each time a relationship went tits up my mum would sigh and say, "I don't know why you don't go out with that nice Luke Wolsey. He's such a lovely lad," with the emphasis on the word '*lovely*'.

"He's always held a torch for you," she'd say, "he would treat you right and would never mess you around."

I never took her advice, of course. Who wants to date someone that their mum actually approves of, right?

It's a terrible cliché but on my 40th birthday I took a good long hard look at my love life and thought what an utter shit show it was. My first marriage had ended in divorce but had produced three beautiful kids so not a total failure.

However here I was ten years into disastrous marriage number two. This relationship was both loveless and now sexless (thank god) to an alcoholic who had threatened to burn the house down with me and my kids in it if I ever left him.

I vividly remember the moment when I told myself that although I wouldn't go looking for love, if it should ever find me again I would grasp it with both hands.

After all those years of my mum harping on about Luke, I considered the possibility that my childhood best friend might well be my Prince Charming.

Luke Wolsey the super doting, well mannered and thoughtful type of man that mums everywhere adored and hoped that someday their daughters would end up marrying.

Ironically the outwardly charming Mr. Wolsey turned out to be the most cruel, devious, manipulative and downright nasty man I have ever known. He very nearly destroyed me and my sanity.

This is my story.

1983

It's the start of year two of secondary school. The head of year walks the new boy into our class. Girls swooned at the pretty well-groomed lad before them, the other boys looked at him and instantly disliked him.

I suppose it came across as jealousy on their part back then. With hindsight I now question whether the lads in my class had the ability to see him for what he truly was, had he collectively triggered a sixth sense amongst them?

Interestingly most lads in the year group thought he was a wanker including Dale, the star player of our school football team who I later went on to briefly date in the final year of school.

Luke didn't care that I had a boyfriend, he continued being his usual flirtatious self much to the annoyance of Dale.

Luke could've had his pick of the girls, however he only had eyes for me.

We quickly became good friends. He hung around with my friendship group which consisted of girls and a few lads who tolerated him for my sake. We would go into town at weekends, or meet up after school.

Did I fancy him? Yeah I suppose I did, but even at thirteen years of age I was conscious of not wanting to spoil our friendship.

He followed me around school like a lost puppy and waited outside my classrooms. He would grab my arse whenever we passed each other in the corridors between lessons. Sounds awful by today's standards, however times were different back then, and it didn't occur to me to be outraged.

He constantly asked me out over the next four years and the years thereafter. The whole year group knew he had a major crush on me, unlike most lads of that age he didn't try to hide it either.

Despite never dating, the Christmas and Valentines' cards from him were always huge lovey dovey ones. They were the kind that came with enormous cardboard envelopes, there were little gifts too.

When coming over to my house he was always very formal and never addressed my mum by her first name. My mum loved this, why do mums fall for that shit??

He would sit outside my house sometimes for hours, wolf whistling or blowing kisses if I happened to glance out of the window.

"How sweet," my mum would coo, I guess I was secretly flattered, if not a bit embarrassed.

This kind of obsessive behaviour perhaps should have served as an early warning sign of things to come. However it was viewed upon as 'sweet love-struck puppy' behaviour by the adults in my family as well as his.

When you left school back in the late 80's, everyone would sign each other's autograph books with good luck quotes and/or saucy messages. The other girls inserted my name and his into some cringey soppy rhyme.

My book mainly consisted of my peers predicting that we would one day be married to each other.

Luke repeatedly said he would 'have' me before I was eighteen.

I would laugh this off followed by 'in your dreams mate!'

1988

I was now eighteen, and he certainly didn't 'have' me. In fact our friendship cooled because I had a 'proper' boyfriend. Luke refused to be friends with me. He stopped taking my calls and wouldn't return the messages I left either.

Before he cooled our friendship, Luke revised his prediction and said he would still 'have' me before I was twenty.

1990

Whilst out one day, I noticed that a car appeared to be following me. However it drove off when I got home, it was just a coincidence I thought. I popped out again a couple of hours later and the same car was back but parked further up my road.

I couldn't see the guy's face as he was wearing a large hat and glasses, I headed towards the vehicle to confront whoever it was. The driver tried to pull away, but luckily for me a bus had blocked him in. Imagine my surprise/shock when I found out that the driver was Luke!

I asked him why he was acting like such a weirdo, why did he not just approach me or knock on my door? He made some bullshit excuse about how he felt embarrassed about how he had behaved a couple of years ago. It seemed feasible enough at the time.

I finally agreed to go on a date with him, although we never actually went anywhere! We would just sit in his car and drive around for hours. Looking back, it was quite bizarre.

I once succeeded in taking him to my local pub. It was only ever the one occasion. He claimed no one liked him and felt people were out to get him. My new friends never really warmed to him anyway due to his flirtatious and cocky manner.

I explained to them that this was just his way and he didn't mean anything by it. I even defended him saying that deep down I thought he was insecure.

Our dating was short lived and only lasted about 2 weeks. It was very innocent, a few kisses, nothing sexual.

It just felt weird dating one of my closest friends and I suggested that we go back to being 'just' friends. He didn't like it, but reluctantly agreed.

Another reason for cutting our relationship short was because I was majorly pissed off that Luke and his dad thought that I needed to 'calm down'. Luke had been chatting to him about how often I went out with my friends to bars and clubs. They were both in agreement that I needed to knock my partying days on the head.

Even when we went back to being just friends, he would never want to socialise as part of a group, it always had to be exclusively me and him. Obviously I now know that he was trying to isolate me from people, but being young and naive I didn't see it then.

He would also turn up at my workplace and telephone my department. Once again those around me thought his actions were 'so cute'

As before Luke repeated his mantra that he would now 'have' me before I was twenty-one.

1991

I had a holiday romance with a lad that I would later marry. Luke took it bad, really bad. In fact he refused all contact with me. I moved away from my home town for several years. I tried to keep up contact with him, however my letters went unanswered my calls never returned.

1997

Luke tracked me down via a mutual friend. He was now married, as was I. Our friendship quickly resumed where it had left off.

Before Facebook there was a website called Friends Reunited. I remember Luke's profile distinctly, it said " After leaving school I became an international porn star, and YES I am still in love with Clare."

I recall saying to him that his wife couldn't have been very happy at this, but he just laughed it off and words to the effect of 'tough'.

After resuming our friendship, we would speak on the telephone or arrange to meet up. He never wanted to meet my husband. He felt that he wouldn't be liked and would feel uncomfortable.

He complained that his wife had tricked him into marriage and that it wasn't a happy one. All of the blame was laid at her door. She was apparently lazy, dowdy and not interested in sex. He was my childhood friend, why would I not believe him?

He asked me straight out if I wanted an affair with him! I told him absolutely not and not to be such a prick!

I only ever met his wife a couple of times. He preferred to keep us apart. He said she didn't like me, so I was surprised when she sent me a friend request on Facebook, He said it was a tactic to spy on him and not to accept.

Knowing what I know now I suspect her request was a friendly gesture rather than a sinister one. Me declining must have came across as hostile to her but a relief to him. Luke had now built a barrier between her, me and the truth about what their marriage was really like.

True to form, Luke declared that he would now 'have' me before I was thirty.

1997-2009
Our friendship continued over the next twelve years. Despite his prediction, he didn't have me before I was thirty.

Never one to give up, he optimistically moved the goal posts to he would have me before I was forty.

We would talk on the phone or text most days, occasionally meet in town for coffee, go to the cinema or he would come round to mine for a Chinese.

I would listen to his marital problems, all of which were allegedly his wife's fault. I would pour out my heart to him about my shit marriage which was beyond saving.

The years of lies and emotional abuse had made me hate my husband.

Luke claimed to have had many opportunities over the years to cheat on his wife. He was always quite cagey about whether he actually did or didn't, probably because of not wanting to tarnish his Mr. Nice Guy persona.

Despite my own shit situation, I still refused to be a sticking plaster for Luke's marriage. I said that I would always listen and be there for him but that was it. I suggested he try counselling to save his marriage, he didn't of course.

2010

I'm now forty, still married but desperately sad and alone. I can't remember the last time I experienced love or affection.

I was also running out of excuses to fob my kids off with as to why their mum was crying....again.

I remember the overwhelming feeling of needing to be loved and held, followed by the panic of possibly never experiencing those kind of emotions again.

I made the decision- there and then- that the next time Luke, or any man, made an advance on me *I would not resist*.

Dec 2010

Several months after my epiphany it actually happened. I don't know who was more shocked; him that after twenty-seven years I had finally fallen for his charms, or me that I had given in. I wasn't proud of myself, I was still married and so was he.

I thought back to years earlier when my husband had deviously waited until the ink was dry on our wedding certificate before revealing his dark past and showing his true colours. Perhaps I should've felt guilt, however the only emotions I experienced were ones of hatred and resentment towards my husband for the lost decade of my life.

I made it clear I expected nothing from Luke, Jesus I had enough complications as it was.

I didn't see him again for nearly three months.

Feb 2011

My husband agreed that we would separate. I had dreamt and fantasised of this moment for years. I'm sure he only agreed to move out as he thought our separation would be temporary.

I was elated to finally be free. I would never again have to dread hearing his key in the lock or shudder as he smashed his fist into a wall or a cupboard, I could breathe again.

March 2011

It was mid March, Luke called out of the blue and said, "I'm back at my mums, I've left Fiona."

To say I was shocked was an understatement. We hadn't talked about this, this was not part of my plan. I actually advised him to take some time out and try to patch things up with FI, he was adamant the marriage was over and there was no going back.

Understandably, I wanted to tread with caution. But this seemed to make him crave me all the more. He was totally besotted and wanted to see me all the time. Sod it I thought, I could be hit by a bus tomorrow why not.

He was gentle, attentive, loving, caring and thoughtful- all the qualities I had been craving. He was the real deal I thought.

I kicked myself for all of those wasted years, life with him was sheer bliss.

Sounds like he adores you my friends would gush. Yes he did adore me and I was so very, very lucky.

He would play the Bruno Mars song 'just the way you are' down the phone to me, he said this was how he felt about me.

We went to fancy restaurants, he lavished me with flowers, perfume and high end clothes. He must have texted me literally hundreds of times during the day every day, plus constant phone calls wanting to know where I was and what I was doing etc. If I didn't reply to his texts within a certain timeframe he got arsey.

He would send: ????

Followed by: helloooooo

And finally: oi .... until I replied to him

I naively thought this was because he loved and cared about me so much.

Luke mentioned he would see other men looking at us when we were out together. He said he got a kick out of their admiring glances because he knew that he was punching way above his weight.

There was something about how he said it though, It made me feel uncomfortable. I felt like a bit of an accessory, I pushed it out of my mind I was just being silly.

He spoke excitedly about 'our future' and where we would live, he asked me to think about what kind of wedding we'd have and the holidays we would enjoy together.

I got on so well with his family, he said they adored me too. Soon I began to receive friend requests from his extended family and his friends including three women within his social circle.

It's not easy making new friends the older you get, I was pleased that they appeared to be so welcoming towards me.

In the months to come, I would find out that these three women were not my friends, they were my enemies- I just didn't know it.

April 2011

I learned more about my best friend in a matter of weeks than I had done over the last twenty-seven years. He had indeed cheated on his wife and many, many times. Did the alarms bells ring for me? Of course not, her unreasonable behaviour drove him to it, I reassured myself.

I was shocked though to find out that he had slept with three of her friends, yes the very same ones that had sent me friend requests! He also socialised with these women and their husbands for christ's sake. I remember thinking *talk about shitting on your own doorstep!*

It transpired that he had actually asked these women to 'friend' me. Now I was aware that he'd slept with them it made me feel uneasy. He said I was being immature and it would look like I was being stand offish if I deleted them. Looking back, I think he got a kick out of having his little harem and thrived on the danger.

It turned out he had also had affairs with his clients. He was a tradesman and would often have to go out of an evening to quote for various building projects. He said it was so easy as Fi was used to him going out quoting for work. She never suspected or questioned a thing, until one client went a bit 'bunny boiler' on him. He said he had managed to smooth things over with her and wriggle out of it.

Strangely he would never talk or discuss these extra marital relationships face to face, it was always on messenger, maybe he felt that he could be more convincing behind a keyboard. Perhaps if we had these chats in person I would see the deceit in his eyes and see him for what he truly was?

He always drummed it into me about the importance of deleting our chat history.

I assured him that I did. Instinct told me to do no such thing.

May 2011
Up until this point it was always him planning our dates and summoning me over to his mum's house. I made the big mistake of suggesting we go out with a couple of my friends, he didn't like it.

"I have looked at these friends' profiles," he said, "One is fuck ugly and the other looks like the honey monster. We can't be seen out with ugly munters, we have to surround ourselves with attractive people only."

I actually thought he was joking- till I saw the look on his face. He was being deadly serious.
I had only suggested going to the bloody cinema, I laughed!
"I don't like planning ahead," he snapped, "You're pushing me and I don't like it."

He then dropped the bombshell.
"You're acting like we are in a relationship," he replied coldly, I felt my stomach lurch.

"What do you mean?" I said, "We are."

I pointed out that HE was the one that had previously mentioned marriage, holidays etc.

"Oh my god, you read so much into stuff and take things literally," he said. "We are just friends with benefits, you're my fuck buddy." He callously laughed.
I felt physically sick. The rug had well and truly been pulled out from under me.
As I drove away from his mum's house he cheerfully shouted 'see ya fuck buddy' as he waved me off.

I don't know how I managed to drive home, I could barely see the road through the tsunami of tears.
I remember feeling so shocked and a total fool.
How had I got it so wrong, believing that we were actually in a relationship, how deluded was I?

Days went by, then a couple of weeks. My messages and calls to him went unanswered, as soon as I logged into FB he would go offline.
I didn't know whether I was coming or going. What had I done wrong? The word fuck buddy went round and round in my head. Had I imagined our relationship? Had I read too much into things?

I would replay our conversations on a loop over and over in my head and analyse them. I scrolled through the thousands of messages.
Yes, he was definitely the instigator but I still doubted myself. I thought I was going insane.

He found out via a FB status that I had been out for a meal with a friend. He suddenly got in touch again, as if nothing had happened. He was his usual charming self.
He casually dropped it in that he didn't like that I had gone out without him, he wanted to know if it was a date, and was relieved when it wasn't.
I played it quite cool with him and wasn't falling for any of his patter. He picked up that the balance of power had shifted between us and for once he was not in total control of the situation.
Not having contact with him for a couple of weeks hurt so bad, I missed him dreadfully. But I also realised that I had started to feel better both mentally and physically for not having him in my life.

He said he still loved and missed me, but quickly followed it up by saying he couldn't make me any promises as he didn't know if he wanted me or not, but did I want to drive over anyway and have a shag?!

I said I deserved better and ended it. I asked him not to contact me again, then logged off the chat.

A day or so later the phone calls started, then the texts, followed by FB messages and emails. I ignored them all, *be strong* I told myself.

As the days went on the calls and messages increased. It was relentless, so much so that I ended up blocking him from everything.

Around this time I received a friend request from Gary Hardy an old school friend. There was no profile pic as such, it was just a pic of a football club, however I noticed that friends of mine were already friends with him so I accepted.

He instantly popped up: *hey Clare, it's been a long time, how are you.*

We chatted for a bit, just small talk really. He popped up again the next day and we had a more lengthy chat.

As the conversation went on his questions were more of a personal nature and a lot more specific. The style and tone of his writing also changed, certain phrases gave the game away.

I hadn't been talking to Gary, I had been talking to Luke!

He denied it of course. *Luke who,* he replied, *I don't even know a Luke*. I ended the conversation there and then and blocked 'Gary"

I contacted the FB friends who had also accepted a request from 'Gary" and explained what had happened and to apologise for Luke duping them just to get to me. Someone who knew the 'real' Gary messaged to say he was fuming that his identity had been used.

The next day I receive another request from Johnny Castle- yep the character from one of my fave films cringe or what?

Obviously it was Luke..... *Why did you have to tell everyone he fumed, people have been messaging me, you have made me look stupid.*

You did that all by yourself, I typed.

What was I supposed to do, he said, *you won't talk to me and have blocked me from everything.*

Leave me alone, after all I'm just a fuck buddy, I said.

Each time I blocked a fake account, Luke opened another. He also began turning up at my workplace.

Two attachments pinged into my inbox. I froze in total shock when I opened them.

They were pics of me. I know what you are thinking, but no they were NOT 'those' type of pics. I knew exactly the moment when he had taken one of them without my consent and the other I couldn't of possibly consented to as I was asleep.

I remembered when I had been getting dressed for work one morning. He was on his phone and looked a bit shifty. I asked him what he was doing and had he just taken a pic of me? 'Don't be daft,' he said, 'I'm just looking at what's going on in FB land.'

I didn't believe him, so he showed me his camera roll. There was no pic, so I let it go despite feeling incredibly uneasy.

He had obviously lied, the pic showed me in my bra and pants and the other I was fast asleep, only he had pulled the duvet down exposing one of my boobs.

I was absolutely raging. Trembling, I unblocked his number and called him to let rip. I ranted and raved but all he could say was, 'what choice had I got, you looked so beautiful and I knew you wouldn't have let me take a pic otherwise.'

Too bloody right, I fumed.

He just couldn't see that he had done anything wrong.

"You showed me your camera roll though and there was nothing there."

He explained that he had emailed himself the pics, then deleted them off of his phone.

"I look at your pics every night," he said, "and kiss them and say ILYTTS. I can't live without you in my life Clare, please give me another chance."

He begged, *I need you I'm a mess.*

I'm ashamed to admit, I took him back.

June 2011

Things were great for a couple of weeks until I was back under his spell. The power I briefly had was now gone, he was back in control again just the way he liked it.

During a trip to town he took me to a posh jewellers.

"I want to get an idea of the sort of engagement rings you like." He said.

Totally confused, I reminded him that he was the one who didn't like planning ahead and freaked out about future plans so I initially refused to go in.

He got his own way, before I knew it we were in the shop, finger sized and ring chosen.

"I'm not buying it today," he said, "I'm going to surprise you when you least expect it. When I propose I want it to be incredible, I've dreamed of this since the very first moment when I walked into your classroom."

Inwardly I felt elated but tried to act cool. Wow, he must really want to be with me I thought. Why else would he do this, perhaps we had now turned a corner in our relationship?

I posted a new profile pic of me, it received a lot of likes and comments.

"Nice pic," he said, "You look lovely even though you can see your wrinkles. Don't worry I still love you though wrinkles and all."

My wrinkles were the little lines everyone gets at the corner of their eyes when they smile. I hadn't noticed them before- now I was suddenly obsessed with them.

Then there were the comments about my curvy bum. Luke had always complimented me on my bum, now he complained that it was just fat.

If I ever dared to challenge him, he would blast 'fat bottomed girls' by Queen on the car stereo to shut me up and bring me to heel. He would joke to his family that the song was actually written about me.

My list of flaws and imperfections were growing by the day.

He criticised everything, from the the way I asked if he would like a drink, to my pronunciation of certain words!

Falling from my pedestal had made my halo well and truly slip.

He was also putting pressure on me to change my hair colour back to light brown; the colour it was when we were at school and to get it permed. I said *absolutely not*, which of course was the wrong answer.

"If you really love me," he said, "You would want to please me and make me happy." He sulked.

It was easier to fob him off than to say no. To buy me some time I lied and said that I would speak to my hairdresser about it, *good girl* he beamed.

If we weren't going out anywhere he would always expect me to visit him at his mum's where he insisted on cooking for us all.

By now I was a nervous wreck. I felt sick all of the time, and had lost 3 stone. Despite the weight loss, the cruel insults about my fat bum continued. My hair was also falling out in clumps.

I dreaded meal times. He would criticise me for holding my fork wrong. Sometimes I forgot and reverted back to my old way. He would glare at my hand from across the table and wouldn't drop his stare until I held my fork the way he wanted me to.

Eating had become a real issue. I could only manage a few mouthfuls because I was in such a bad way. He would not let me leave the table until I cleared my plate. He and his family would go and watch TV, leaving me sat at the table like a naughty child. When I did finish I was praised with 'good girl' and a kiss on my head.

He only ever let me cook for him on one occasion. Despite putting a lot of effort into the meal, he pulled a face and said it was 'edible'.

He was horrified that I had cut the carrots into rings- apparently this is so common, who knew? Carrots should be julienne or batons he lectured me.

I casually mentioned that next time I would make slow cooked beef stew and dumplings. I was quickly put in my place, 'there won't be a next time, you will never cook or serve me peasant food,' he said.

He had become very secretive, always holding his phone, taking it to the loo with him, messages constantly pinging away.

Sally, one of his customers, was always messaging him especially late at night. If I dared to question it I was accused of being neurotic and possessive.

"I can't handle your lack of trust," he complained. "You're mental, it's all in your head."

Weeks later I had confirmation that he had screwed her, but he still had the arrogance to deny it.

If I had the option of going out with a friend, he would suddenly show interest in wanting to come over to my place. He would never turn up though. I would just be left sitting there wondering what was going on?
Obviously he had absolutely no intentions of coming round, he just wanted me to think that he was so I would stay in instead of going out.
As well as screwing Sally (and god knows who else) I also found out that he had been sleeping with his estranged wife for months. Every bouquet of flowers or bottle of perfume hadn't been a gift out of love, it had been to ease his conscience.

Family and friends were now expressing concern about my fragile, skeletal appearance (I thought I looked ace). One of my friends described me as looking like a lollipop. They begged me to finish with him, but I wouldn't.
They didn't have to worry though as Luke ended our relationship, due to me questioning him over Sally amongst other things. He said he couldn't put up with me not trusting him anymore, I was a mess.

July 2011
Whenever we broke up, I noticed a pattern of behaviour.

He would initially ignore me completely, but then after a while his lack of control over what I was doing would prove to be too much for him and he would test the water with a text message.

I was determined to stay strong this time. The more I blanked him the more the harassment intensified. He got his family members to call me, I never picked up.

They would also send FB messages asking me to talk to him, claiming he was a mess, they were concerned for his health as they had never seen him so depressed.

One afternoon whilst at work, I was ambushed by him and four members of his family. His mum took me aside hugged me and begged me not to shut him out- the fucking cheek of it! She said it was me that he wanted, but if I carried on refusing to speak to him this would push him back into the arms of Fi - how low was that?

She asked me to give him more time, wait for him and to take his calls.

I couldn't believe it when she remarked how thin I was. "Her Luke" didn't like it that I had lost my curves and no longer had an arse- the very same arse he had drummed into me was fat!!!

Despite being caught off guard, I was so bloody strong. I told her straight that she had no right to ask that of me. I had to put my kids and me first and move on with my life. I had given Luke months and many chances, this time I was done.

My words fell on deaf ears, his harassment continued. However, I stayed strong.

I was working the late shift one Friday evening, when he turned up again, alone this time. He opened his mouth to deliver a no doubt carefully rehearsed speech. but I raised my hand in a gesture that said, *don't bother mate I ain't interested.*

He quickly pulled a ring box out of his pocket, it was the ring box from the jewellers where we chose my ring. It completely floored me. I was not expecting or prepared for that!

I didn't stick around to see what he would do next. I repeated my request to be left alone and walked away to find my manager who was also my friend.

I broke down in Jay's office and between sobs I told him about what had just happened. He dashed downstairs to throw Luke out of the building himself, but thankfully he'd already gone.

Jay and I walked to our cars after the shift ended a few hours later. My heart stopped when I saw Luke sitting on the floor of the car park, his back leaning against my driver's door. Jay protectively took me into his car and drove me from his parking space to mine. He told Luke to leave me alone, and that he would be calling the police if he carried on harassing me at work.

He scuttled off like the coward that he was.

August 2011

The calls and texts contlnued. He wrote me a long message explaining how he was a broken man, he went on to declare his undying love for me blah blah blah. He mentioned he'd had got his kids for the day, and that they were sad because he was upset and were asking 'daddy why are you crying'. What kind of a shit uses his kids for emotional blackmail?

He said that this would be the last time he would contact me. If I didn't reply by the end of the day, he would leave me alone to get on with my life and would never bother me again.

He had never said that before, his words sounded so final this time. Was this really the end of the road?

I guess the dirty trick of using his kids must have had the desired effect on me as I suddenly felt desperately sorry for him. I pictured his kids and their little sad faces full of concern for their beloved daddy.

An overwhelming wave of sadness washed over me.

I decided that I would call him (I know, I know I'm a muppet) I would call him on Tuesday, I thought, make him sweat a couple more days I told myself. As if that really made a difference in the grand scheme of things.

Tuesday came and I called him. The chat was brief and to the point. I laid out my terms for taking him back, he agreed to everything. He was over the moon to have me once again. He wanted to meet up but I said no, for once he didn't push me.

Throughout the day I had thought of more questions that I needed answers to, so I called him several times that evening. Each time his phone rang out.

The next morning I woke up to a FB message from Fi it read: "stop calling him, he's spending the night with me."

Un-fucking-believable!!! He shits on me the very day that I agree to give him another chance, how fucking stupid have I been???

My mobile rings, it's him all bright and cheerful, morning treacle tits he says. Sorry I missed your calls, I was so knackered after work I just crashed out.
I can't believe how calm I was.

"Fi has told me you spent the night with her," I said. True to form he was more disgusted that Fi had royally dropped him in it rather than being ashamed at being caught with his pants down on the very day I stupidly agreed to give him another chance.

I told him that was it, I was done - for real this time. I actually felt relief more than I did anger.

I was curious though, I wanted to know why he had gone to the effort of getting his family to plead his case plus turning up at my work with an engagement ring if he was just going to carry on being a shit?

"What are you going on about?" he said, "Why would you think I had got you a ring?"

"You turned up at my work with the ring box from the jewellers where we chose a ring," I replied.

He started laughing, "Oh bless you," he said patronisingly, "You really thought I had actually got you a ring!" He was belly laughing now, and I felt so foolish. *I can't believe you would think that*, he laughed.
I felt so small and stupid.
He explained that the box was empty apart from a piece of paper with the word PROMISE which he had written on it. The 'promise' was that it was me that he wanted- how pathetic!

"Goodbye, Luke." I hung up.
I messaged his family members with the latest developments and asked them not to contact me in the coming weeks or come to my place of work begging me to take him back. I then unfriended them.

October-geddon
I was doing ok-ish. He contacted me a couple more times (which I knew he would) one occasion he was feeling sorry for himself, very 'woe is me" and arrogantly assumed I would fall for it once the dust had settled- I didn't.
I can't handle this, was his pathetic response.
'No, you can't handle getting caught,' was my reply.
He went for my jugular.

I've still got the pictures Clare, he said coldly, *they are on my hard drive with the others. I can look at you anytime I want.*

He wouldn't divulge what 'others' meant. Did he mean pics of me that I didn't know were being taken or pics of other women? To this day I still do not know, the not knowing eats away at me.

A family member went to the police for advice about the photos. As understanding as they were they said there wasn't a great deal that they could do as he would just deny still having them if questioned. However, should Luke ever share or post these pictures he could then be prosecuted.

He would never do that (I hope) it just makes me feel sick to think of him perving over me. Even if he did post them online he would look like a total sleazebag, because anyone with half a brain cell can see from the pics that I had no idea that they were being taken.

Of the three ladies that friended me, I would only really chat to one. I always got the feeling that she was just 'sussing me out' to see what I knew rather than being polite. She asked straight if I knew about her and Luke?

One thing's for sure she certainly didn't know about the other two.

Understandably all three were angry and worried that Luke had blabbed about his conquests.

All four of us shared one thing in common, we were fragile and broken when he moved in on us. He was a cold blooded serial predator. He had the ability to sense a women's vulnerability the same way a shark senses blood. He exploited us at our lowest, circling us, feeding off of our sadness and despair before moving in for the kill.

Just when I thought it couldn't get any worse, I received a strange message from a mutual acquaintance asking me if I was ok and did I need help?

It must have terrified Luke that one day the truth might come out. So he decided to get his story in first and told Fi and the others that I was having a breakdown, that I was mentally unhinged and a woman scorned.

He warned Fi that I might come out with some bat shit crazy lies that he had slept with her pals!! He shamelessly roped the other three in to back him up, to say that I was nuts and to save his own skin, certainly not theirs.

As angry as I felt I did understand why these women went into warrior mode, they were just trying to protect their relationships and friendships, they had a lot to lose...........BUT

Something snapped in me.

How dare they make out that I was some sort of lunatic. I could have handled being called anything else, seriously I would have put my big girl pants on and just sucked it up. But to make out that I was mentally deranged, to save his own hairy arse was the final straw.

I decided that I would finish this once and for all, and I now didn't give a fuckity fuck who got caught in the crossfire.

I printed off transcripts of all of the conversations, the ones that I promised him I had deleted. I armed myself with a highlighter pen and set to work. There was so much damning info that it took me about a week.

In his own words it detailed how he had: slept with her friends, slept with clients, the lies he had told over the years when she grew suspicious, how she was to blame for tricking him into marriage, asking me not to accept her friend request and a whole lot more.

I posted it off.

If she wanted to take him back then good luck to her.

However, I wanted her to be in full position of the facts. The man that she thought she knew didn't exist, he was an illusion. He only let her see what he wanted her to see. She had been living a total lie with a predator that was a danger to women.

They got back together, but not for long. I don't know if reading about his cheating in his own words haunted her and this eventually brought her to her senses or if he left her?

I felt guilty for a long long time and regretted what I had sent to her, maybe her ignorance was bliss?

I confess to checking her FB occasionally over the years. I genuinely wanted to know that she was doing ok. Any reservations or remorse I felt about sending the evidence of his serial cheating to her dispersed when I saw how happy she looked.

She has indeed moved on, and has been with the same man for years now.

I know FB pics can give a false perception of a person's life, however you can't fake the happiness in her eyes. She really does look radiant, I'm so pleased for her- god knows she deserves a happy ending after being married and controlled by that pig.

Despite everything that happened, Luke did not learn a damn thing. Proof that a leopard can never change its spots.

After Fi took him back that final time, he rewarded her by having another affair- all whilst trying to reel me back in as well!! I'm reliably informed that he made this latest victim very ill too.

I'm sure he still spies on me from time to time. He found out a few years ago that I had met someone and arrogantly sent a friend request to my new partner.
If it was done to unnerve me and to let me know that he was still watching from the shadows... it worked.

My experience goes to show that do we ever truly know anyone?

Leave You Behind

By Lindzi aged 15

I think it hurt when I did you wrong,
But it hurt me more when you had gone,
You made it worse, you kept leading me on.
Until my feelings had grown so strong.

For three months or more, I wanted you here.
My only wish was to hold you near.

Over and over again you messed me around.
Building me up and then letting me down.

The crazy thing was, I would still do,
Any-thing you asked me to.

I kept coming back, over again,
Putting up with the lies and the pain.

No one else could understand,
The way I felt under your command.

Sometimes you made me feel good, but then you'd rip
me apart.
Destroying my world and breaking my heart.

I only had to see your cloudy brown eyes,
And it was like you had me hypnotised.

I never cared what others did or said.
I could not get it into my head;

That me and you together would never be the same,
Because all it was to you was a spiteful game.

After believing I could not go on without you anymore,
I knew I had to get myself over you for sure.

So I didn't go to see you and instead I kept away.
And it began to get easier, day by day.

Then from you I received a call,
Saying you did still love me after all.

I found it strange and a bit hard to believe,
That you only decided this when I was ready to leave.

But despite my suspicion, your words I obey,
And go over to your house anyway.

At first your words were, oh so kind.
And once again, my love was blind.

Once you had me back, you re-started your game so cruel,
And I realised I had been such a fool!

But again I found out when it was too late.
You had already put me into such a state.

I thought of you, all of the time.
Wishing that you would only be mine.

I had friends to help me, although they couldn't do much.
Because they couldn't stop me from craving your touch.

Then I met someone else, so happy and bright.
And at the end of the tunnel there was suddenly a light.

I realised it wasn't love before. It hadn't been so true.
And now all I felt was pity for you.

The fact you hadn't wanted me, had made me want you more,
But now I know you just acted immature.

It was your loss now, I couldn't believe I'd been so blind.
And now I was going to leave you behind.

Better Off Fishing
By Lindzi aged 33

Girl you got it bad for dick heads and for narcs,
Back then you managed to find them by just hanging around on parks.

And a mistake you made then- and continued for too long…
Was moving straight on! And ignoring your gut whilst seeking out the wrong.

Healing is hard. But you can fix the pain.
Then you'll forget about it and do it all again!

But, listen here, do not fear being alone.
The times you've been solo have been the times you've really grown.

It really doesn't help that the bad taste in men still exists.
And I still fall for it, even now and knowing the risks.

So I'm not here to preach, I just want you to know,
You should just be yourself, go with the flow and allow your energy to glow.

You are enough. If someone says that you're not,
Leave them behind, they'll soon be forgot,

Try not to regret, always develop and learn.
What I'm realising by now, is these wrinkles I earn.

Seeking Appointment

After severe dissatisfaction with her previous supplier over many years, failure to keep promises and outright fraud, Helen Johnson, is happy to announce she is putting out to tender applications for the post of her next lover(s).

There will be a very strict vetting procedure.

Applicants must be able to demonstrate that they can provide polite (but raunchy) sex, pleasant chat and should have a sense of humour and be able to tell funny stories, the ability to give good head is not negotiable.

The successful applicant/s (there are several positions available) will have to take part in a series of interviews.

These interviews will be conducted in a public space to begin with, where applicants may, once they have shown a proper interest in the humanity of Ms Johnson, be allowed a kiss and arm stroke. Eye contact is welcome.
Applicants who try to rush Ms Johnson and to advance the selection process will find themselves having to restart the process once more.

With subsequent interviews, communication may be conducted electronically but only to confirm basic details like time of appointment, location of interview and so on.
Only very light teasing and flirting may be allowed electronically. Save the real flirting for the interviews.
Dick pics/sexting will not be tolerated under any circumstances.

The interviews are a two way process.

Ms Johnson will want to get to know you as a person. She will be particularly interested in candidates that show a little vulnerability. An ex may be discussed in passing, especially if they share a child. However continued slagging off of an ex no matter how horrible she may have been will demonstrate to Ms Johnson that you are not ready to move on or have mummy issues.
If the ex is discussed in such a way that is insulting to all women, Ms Johnson will end the selection process.

Deeper interviews: Once Ms Johnson decides that your intentions are honourable but sexy, she will conduct intimate one to one interviews behind closed doors in her bedroom. In this interview you must be on your best behaviour, remember chaps if Ms Johnson doesn't like what you are doing then you must stop. Consent is an ongoing process. In these interviews you will be party to what you may expect should your application be successful.

This first interview may not go as you had planned.
Do not fear, Ms Johnson has experienced this from previous suppliers. If a deep interview goes badly because of nerves do not worry you are still in the running for the position. Refrain from overeating and over indulging in alcohol for your next interview. You may feel that you do not want to try the second interview, fear not. Previous holders of the post(s) were not put off by a failure to perform and came back triumphantly.

Finally, if at the end of the interviewing process you feel the job is not for you, then you must say so regretfully and politely.

Thank Ms Johnson for her time and go on your way. If, at a future date you are feeling lonely and in need of a shag then you will have to start the interview process once more. You may not go straight to the deeper interview at this stage.

The successful candidate will be able to experience mind blowing blow jobs, discover erogenous zones they didn't know existed and find a deep erotic satisfaction from a top class milf.

In addition, outside the bedroom, Ms Johnson is a superb cook. She can make you the dish you dreamed of from your childhood that reminds you of your grandmother.

Ms Johnson is talented, creative, funny, affectionate and warm. Ms Johnson has a deep interest in people and if you are successful she will continue to like and respect you as a man.

If you treat her like a lady, she will treat you like a stud. Your self esteem will soar in your new job, Ms Johnson is a very experienced life coach and will offer suggestions of how you can improve relations with your family and in your profession.

In your job you will be expected to communicate and discuss things that are not going well. You don't have to beat your chest, you are a male human not a gorilla. If you continue to show genuine interest in Ms Johnson and offer encouragement and allow her to grow, you will experience growth as well.

However, if you try to control Ms Johnson, if you belittle her achievements or call them "cute", if you engage in any of the following you will be fired immediately:

Devaluing
Silent treatment
Belittling
Criticising Ms Johnson's driving is a big no no

Ms Johnson doesn't care about cars, cars are just machines like vacuum cleaners get over yourself

Twinkle in eye and confidence with a little bit of vulnerability is ideal

Showing off of any type does not impress Ms Johnson forget what you have seen in the movies

Ms Johnson is impressed by quiet confidence, let her discover your achievements piece by piece

Loving and affectionate

Good looks not necessary if you have the above

Age range 38-65 (some flexibility)
Financially independent
Educated
English or French speaking
Absolutely no electronic engineers
No right wingers
No addictions (if former addict must have got clean long time ago with lots of therapy)

No narcs

Narc in the Home

By Cippy

I met AF when I was 17. He was handsome, gorgeous in fact. He was older than me, more mature! More importantly, he had a car!

We dated, I ended up pregnant... we got engaged and bought a house. Life was bloody good.

And then we got the Internet. He met her online. I had no idea. Eventually he got the balls to tell me he'd been chatting to a woman from India and that she wanted to visit. Distraught, I figured it would be a fling and he would come right back to me. In hindsight, I was a fool for love.

She came over for two weeks...we were all friends, we went on day trips, out for meals. When she went home I figured life would return to normal.

How wrong was I!

She would chat to me online, comment on my pretty hair and tell me any man would be lucky to have me. In the next breath she would tell me I was a waster and that I didn't deserve a family and that she would run it better.

I stupidly agreed with AF that we could sponsor her work visa.

She moved in. I moved into my daughter's room. I'd come home from work to meals cooked for AF and my daughter, none for me.

She would clean my house after I'd done it, telling me what a terrible housewife I was, asking me how I expected to keep a man if I couldn't run a house! I was working full-time and caring for a three year old!

She would continually brag about her education and belittle me for being "common" or working class.

She spent a great deal of time trying to prove she was better than me, prettier and more educated. She loved the sound of her own voice.

She had two sides; the nice side scared me the most.

She would be super sweet and nice. Tell me she was proud of how grown up I was handling the situation.

She would be picture perfect for anyone who came round or when we were out in public. She would never flaunt a physical relationship with AF in my face, she would always give me a peck on the cheek goodnight!

By this point she had successfully got me isolated from friends and family. People knew where to find me if I took my own life!

The last straw for me was after a rare night out with friends. I'd agreed to let my daughter stay home with them.

I came home to underwear on the lounge floor. They should have been babysitting not rutting in front of the fireplace!

I lost my shit, broke some of her teeth! Gave them twenty-four hours to leave.

What I hadn't expected was just how much of a god complex she had.

She told me that she was a better mother to my daughter, that they would be having my home and that I wouldn't win against her ever.

She laughed telling me stealing my man was just the start, she would have my life, my daughter and my home. She told me that I have no self respect and that I didn't deserve to be in my daughter's or AF's life and that she would take care of them.

Thanks to amazing friends and a good solicitor that didn't happen. Though she manipulated me into buying AF out rather than rinsing him, using my adoration for him... I couldn't see him homeless etc.

It was turbulent for many years.

My daughter would visit them. I wasn't allowed their address. I didn't argue... I was too beat down. When they collect my lil one, AF wouldn't be allowed in the house.

In later years, she tried to be my friend. This would usually happen after AF was late or hadn't turned up to school plays. My daughter was always disappointed and she would say things like.... *oh you know what he's like*.

AF got pretty sick about eight years ago. She couldn't hack it and desperately needed support.

Stupidly I ended up taking her to the hospital or visiting him whilst she was god knows where.

They married... she's fucking the neighbour.

I'll always worry about sharing such a story as I sound like a jealous ex. I loved and adored AF. He was a peter pan. He will never grow up, he would never show emotions.

I was very bitter for a long time. Being told how to behave by another woman is belittling.

I hated her. Now I pity her.

Ask Everyone.

By DP

"Ask everyone," he says,
"They all think the same," he says.
"You're this, you're that, you're all the things bad."

So I apologise.
But it's not enough.
It never is.

"What more do you want from me?" I ask,

"I want you to be sorry."
"I've said sorry so many times already."
"No you haven't, you don't mean it."
"I do mean it, I'm sorry."
Never quite sure if I'm the one who's meant to be apologising.

"Ask everyone."

"Ask everyone."

"Ask everyone," he says.

So I did.

And I stopped apologising.
They didn't think I was this, or that.
None of the bad things he called me came from them.
The lies he surrounded me with started to crumble.
And the truth was.
He was all of those things.
Not me.

Narc Shark

By Lurcherlass

I lost my father on June 2nd 2017 suddenly and on Aug 2nd 2017, I tragically lost my husband after a traumatic year of illness. Shortly after that, in December, a good friend was buried too.

I was vulnerable and exceedingly lonely, walking the house at night and not eating.

I decided the best I could do was join a dating site as at least that way I could talk to people.

Unfortunately about three months in I met a guy, a little younger than me who lived locally and started a relationship with him. He quickly moved in with me and life seemed good again. I lent him £10,000 to buy a car he wanted...how stupid. That December we went abroad for a holiday and if I'm honest, I look back and think I should have realised then he was starting to manipulate me.

Some of the things he did. Say if I left my keys on the worktop when I'd go to get them, they wouldn't be there. He would tell me I'd put them somewhere else so slowly I started thinking maybe it was me. He started telling me it was my age and I was probably getting dementia.

He never answered his phone or texts until it suited him and sometimes I could not get hold of him at all.

I've since found out he was seeing someone he had a child with. She warned me not to get involved with him as he was a narcissist and gas lighter.

I chose to ignore her. I wish I'd listened.

If I drove when we went out he would tell me my driving wasn't good and would question the routes I chose so I began asking which way to go. His reply then would be, *you're driving you decide.*

I began to lose confidence in everything I did as he would criticise me. He dominated the TV remote when he was in, saying it was his TV (he got rid of mine when he moved in and replaced it with a bigger one!)

If I initiated sex he would ask me what the hell I thought I was playing at but was then happy to wake me at 2.30am to satisfy his sexual needs.

We went on holiday again around March after I was very ill. He refused to get out of bed until lunchtime or later and always wanted booze straight away.

He had refused to go half or full board so I nearly always ended up hungry as I had to wait for him or he would sulk. The week was awful but I was, by this time, afraid to say much as it caused arguments and he would just walk out.

We decided to go on holiday again later in the year. Having packed ready to go we went out for something to eat the night before leaving. On arriving home, as usual he wanted to go to the pub, and I decided to go too. He wasn't pleased. When we got our drinks he told me to sit at the table and not speak unless I had something urgent to say.

The following morning I was up early to sort things out as we were due to fly at 4.15pm. He stayed in bed until 1. I had asked if he wanted me to book a taxi but he said he would sort it. He then disappeared. I finally got a phone call at 2pm to ask me to sort a taxi which I did.

When we arrived at the train station to catch a connection to Manchester Airport we had missed it.

I mentioned we probably wouldn't make the flight and he flew into a rage and left me on the platform, returning just as the later train did. We just made check in.

Not being a seasoned traveller, I had asked where to put different things i.e. hold not hand luggage and when I had things taken off me by security as they should have been in hold, he told me off saying he had said that's where they should have been. No way did he.

He then wanted a drink in a bar so I followed to be told to go and sit and read somewhere as the flight was delayed. I refused. They didn't have his normal so I pointed out another drink and he flew at me saying if he wanted to know he'd ask the barman.

I realised at that point I was not going anywhere with him, certainly not abroad so I refused to fly and asked him for my spending money back which I'd given him in the morning to get Euros with. He made me stand and wait whilst he slowly drank a pint before flinging it at me.

I went home after a friend collected me as I'd gone into meltdown. I wanted to commit suicide that night I was so miserable.

The pills were on the side but something made me stop and Google to make sure I would die... I wouldn't but I would have been in hospital a very long-time.

Never heard a word all week from him but the following weekend he appeared and he looked awful, even my friend felt sorry for him so knowing he hadn't anywhere to stay I let him have the spare room... silly me! Obviously in time we got back together.

He started staying out the odd nights with no real excuse so I decided I really had had enough so I packed his things and told him to collect them.

He refused.

I told the police what I had done.

He came round as he needed his work's iPhone which he had inadvertently left at mine. To cut a long story short he couldn't take all his stuff so the police asked me to keep one box overnight which happened to contain said phone.

When I picked it up it had a message from his next 'victim ' so I phoned her to tell her all about him. She didn't believe me and carried on seeing him.

Fast forward a few months, he supposedly had finished seeing her and I moved and we got back together yet again.

How stupid can one person be?

He came in one night whilst I was out and took my TV and DVD player and I have since found out he gave it to his next lady.

He has intermittently texted me threats which I ignore and she now has also finished with him.

We got our heads together and worked it out that if he wasn't with me he had been with her and if he wasn't with either of us he was with two other women he's had children with.

He got violent towards her, kicking her door in when she refused to have him back.

It is incredibly hard to prove coercion and even though the police took a three hour statement, they decided there just wasn't enough to get a definite prosecution.

I look back now and see I was so desperate to be loved and so vulnerable after my darling husband died, I was such an easy target for this guy.

I've lost more money in two years than I dare think about but at least I'm still alive.

The next one lost money too although not as much as me.

He's already back on dating sites after the next lady finished with him. She put on a false profile the day after they finished and he was trying to date her... how ironic!

Cheats Never Prosper

By Gary Clarke

I sit here feeling all hurt and destroyed.
How you left suddenly has left a void.

A pain in my chest, my heart is aching.
Watching you leave, a part of me you're taking.

But nothing left of you, just destroyed photos.
Of happy times together, I know you know.

I see the ash at the bottom of the garden,
Burning this life of us you now pardon.

But mine will stay in my mind forever,
Of my affair I didn't want you to discover,
She was just my mistress, she weren't my lover,
I jumped in the deep end, thinking of no other.

You cried, you shouted, you wished we hadn't met,
You told me you're leaving and you to forget.

How can I forget the love of my life?
The one that agreed to forever be my wife.

I destroyed your heart and also broke mine,
Me and my cheating I could never define.

I just wish one day you'll forgive me for this,
I'm sorry you're leaving me with never a kiss.

My Story

By DP

There's so much I want to write, I don't know where to start. All I know is that from where I am now, looking back on the entire relationship from a place of safety and refuge, I realise that the red flags were there from the start.

It's easy to say from the outside, "Why did you put up with him for so long?"

But when you're stuck inside the manipulation, the lies, the love bombing, the gas lighting- it is impossible to see, and the excuses for him just roll off the tongue.

He's not an abuser. It's just the way he is, and the good things outweigh the bad, don't they? Yes he has a drinking problem, and he spends too much of our money on cocaine- but I've joined in in the past so can I really stand on my high horse?

He never laid a finger on me; that was my limit.

The moment he did I would end things, but that just gave him free reign to abuse me in many other ways.

Every argument we had ended in him threatening to split up.

"It's over," he would yell, amongst every swear word you could imagine. I've been called it all.

Even when he was at fault, I'd be the one who ended up apologising, feeling confused and guilty and not knowing why as he'd talk rings around me, twisting everything I'd say and jumping on any contradiction he'd manage to whittle out of me.

I can say exactly when it started changing for me.

A new life growing inside me was the beginning of the end of our relationship.

It wasn't just me that would have to deal with and accept it as normal life now. My priorities shifted but I still couldn't leave. Not while I was pregnant, where would I go? How could I afford it?

Surely he'll change once baby is here, right? I've got to hold on for that hope. He's told me he will stop after this weekend. Next month will be different. I'll just wait and see.

It took over a year after our beautiful baby arrived for the final penny to drop that no, things would never change. Not unless I changed them.

I did it. I ended it.

My child will not grow up seeing this is the way a man speaks to a woman; or anybody speaks to anybody else for that matter.

My child will not grow up thinking that drinking every day is normal. My child will not grow up to turn into a clone of their father.

Three Cats Later

By Ellie Finch

My story is dedicated to Benjamin Hutchinson- the man who taught me how to laugh again.

I met Dave (not his real name) in my second year at university. He was a member of the society I had just joined, a master's student at the Uni, and was intelligent, hard-working, and seemed fun. Dave changed my life, permanently.

I should have spotted the warning signs. When we met he was friends with a girl who stayed over at his place a couple of days each week, in his spare room. It seemed that everywhere he went, she went. At the time I had no interest in him as a partner, it seemed that he was already taken, and I have no interest in breaking up a couple, but the situation seemed odd so I asked him about it.

He claimed she was obsessed with him, and was struggling to accept that they were only ever going to be friends.

He'd slept with her once, over a year ago, but had decided that they just didn't connect enough to be more than friends. He felt sorry for her so didn't have the heart to tell her that he didn't want her around. As he spilled out his worries and concerns over the next few weeks and months, we got closer.

By now I was more than convinced that they were not in a relationship, and never would be, but felt sorry for the girl as I knew that eventually, he would have to be honest with her and hurt her.

Eventually we got together, although unofficially as he still didn't want to hurt his friend. As a result, our relationship had to be kept secret, until it was the right time to tell her about it, so as to reduce the hurt she would suffer. It took three months before he "told her", and the fallout from that should have clued me in- but I trusted him.

I had no idea why this girl was so upset about it, when (according to him) they'd only ever been friends, but I really felt for her. I trusted that he was telling me the truth. I shouldn't have.

Three months after the other girl left, the news of our "official" status dropped. His friends- who soon became my friends- were delighted. Swept up in the happy feelings, I soon forgot the other girl and her "obsession", and even when I did think of her it was with pity that she was so mistaken in her belief that they were more than friends.

I'd waited a long time to make our relationship official, and I wanted to enjoy every moment of that "honeymoon" phase.

Initially everything seemed to be going smoothly, aside from his unwillingness to commit to anything. But there were... little things. Little signs, that I ignored. Things that I swept under the rug in an attempt at keeping this man, whom everyone agreed treated me like a princess and was a catch.

I had noticed that something was a bit off with his mum.

The first time I met her was about six months into the relationship. She lived in Kent and therefore her visits were infrequent. I'd met her briefly the evening before, and she had cried and held him like she thought he was dying. I'd stayed over at his that night to offer support as she seemed quite distressed.

We were getting "busy" that morning, not having had time the night before due to all the upset, when suddenly the door opened and she burst in. Dying from embarrassment I'd dressed and left via the back door, not able to meet her again, knowing what she had seen. When I next saw him he told me that she had thought he was crying and had come in to comfort him- even at the time I was incredulous about this, but how do you say to someone that you're pretty sure their mum walked in on them on purpose?

The next time she visited there was a repeat of her crying. It didn't take me long to realise that this was her thing. She did it to gain his attention and he always diverted all his time and attention to her during these visits.

I tried to avoid her as much as was possible. In addition to her crying was the way she would make little comments that put me down, about the way I tidied up or where I stored things. She once even gave me a dressing down about where I stored my plant food (apparently under the kitchen sink is NOT an appropriate location.)

It was lots of little, petty insignificant things but it was enough to constantly make me feel like I wasn't good enough for *her* son, that I was lacking in some way.

His mum's visits I could deal with though. She was only ever around for a week or two, and then life could return to normal. His Mad Mum became something my own mum and I would joke about in order to help me cope while she was around. I would store up stories about the crazy behaviour she exhibited and re-tell it later on and we'd all have a chuckle. Like the time I mentioned to her that I would love to go to the botanical gardens but couldn't at that moment as I was studying hard for finals, so as soon as Dave walked into the room she said to him, "I'd love to go to the botanical gardens – shall we do that today?". And then they left, taking a couple of our mutual friends to the very place I had just told her I would love to visit. I now know where he learnt his behaviour.

This was when more significant events started happening.

There was an occasion where I was working in a group to create an exhibition for a module at Uni. I had asked Dave for help and he agreed, coming into Uni to help set the exhibition up.

One of my more bumbling lecturers had come over to offer advice and help and had pulled at one of the divider screens, accidentally tearing it and creating more work. Accidents happen. But Dave lost it.

He shouted at my lecturer and stormed out- I was mortified.

I can't adequately explain the shock and embarrassment I felt in front of my peers and lecturers, knowing that the story would be passed around. It was the first time he'd slipped in front of people outside the relationship- probably because these people didn't matter to him.

But I put it aside, thinking it was a one off. I had already learnt not to confront him.

I feel that at this point I need to make a couple of things clear.

Firstly, I am not in any way, shape or form a naturally quiet, meek kind of person. I know what I want and I get it. I work hard, I'm intelligent, I fight rather than flight, I'm stubborn and I try to be kind to as many people as I can, and I always try to do the right thing, as opposed to the easy thing.

People seem to have an image of the traditionally "beaten wife" in their head as being a meek little thing, long-suffering, perhaps a little stupid and definitely someone from a poor background, a woman wearing rags with a dirt floor under her feet – the Cinderella of abuse. Of course, this is not true.

Abuse can happen to anyone.

Abusers can BE anyone.

Secondly, Dave was never, ever violent. He never shouted, he never called me names, until the end when he was losing control and getting desperate.

His methods were far more subtle than that.

When he was displeased he could make my life a living hell, like walking over broken glass. His bad moods and tempers could last for weeks. He would subtly insinuate that I was lacking in intelligence or that my standards were not good enough. That *I* was not good enough.

He had made it fixed in my head that he was punching down in our relationship, that he'd done me a favour by getting rid of the other girl in the beginning to be with me, and that I was nowhere near good enough to be his girlfriend. I had managed to get an amazing man, who was so much better than I was as a person- more intelligent, more kind, more thoughtful, a man who was going to go far and do amazing things. And I was lucky enough that he had decided to lower his standards and let me come along for the ride. But I had to make up for what I was lacking.

Therefore, everything had to be done his way. We had to hang out with *his* friends (who were better than my own friends) we had to do *his* hobbies. When we moved in together, he had his own separate bedroom because he needed his own space, where I couldn't "control" him, as if I was a controlling sort of person.

My dreams and ambitions were put to the side and ignored.

I was told that we would never own a cat because *he* didn't want one. We wouldn't be getting married because *he* didn't believe in marriage.

When, after I'd finished Uni and wanted to move further away from the students and start living as an adult, he wanted to stay – he wouldn't even leave the Society we'd met at, despite the newcomers being 18 year old students and him being 27 and in full time employment.

I wanted to move out of shared accommodation, but that was also rejected. I couldn't even get him to commit to buying a new TV, ditching the old CRT ginormous box we had, and one time I mentioned going on holiday together... let's say I never bothered suggesting it a second time.

But whatever he wanted was what we did, and while we appeared like the perfect, loving couple from the outside, things were getting worse on the inside.

However, he was starting to slip up more frequently.

He once started to have a proper go at me when we were at a local bar with his friends about my smoking. It was the one thing that really got to him. He couldn't make me quit. He was really going for me, making me feel inadequate and like a failure- stressing that he would never normally date a smoker but he had made an exception because he thought I would be capable of quitting and I had promised that I would. The threat of him leaving me hung in the night air like the pressure before a storm.

He was doing it in front of his friends too. It got so bad that his best friend stood up for me, telling Dave to, "Leave it".

I've never felt more grateful to anyone in all my life.

That was all it took. Dave had to constantly look like he was an amazing person in front of his friends. I could feel the anger vibrating inside him, but not another word was mentioned about it.

The mood it put him in lasted for weeks. His air of "putting up with me" intensified and I was terrified of losing him, until eventually things returned to the previous status quo, although he was very careful to not slip in front of his friends again.

One of the strange little things he did to keep up the appearance of being the perfect boyfriend happened every time someone took a photo of us. When the photo was taken, he would always be staring at me with an adoring look on his face, while I was looking at the camera. It always made me feel so uncomfortable – I don't like things that feel fake, and it always felt like an act that was put on for those around us.

People would see the photos and comment that he "really loved me" – of course this got twisted in my head, that I didn't love him enough, that I should have been the one staring at HIM with adoration, after all, he's lowered himself to my level, not the other way around.

I dare say that the people who made the comments about how much he clearly loved me would be mortified by how my mind twisted their meaning, but by that point I had been trained to think like that – it wasn't their fault.

I started to notice that the friendship between him and another mutual friend of ours was starting to get very close.

She and her partner had been our friends for a year or so. I liked her bubbly personality and her partner was just as geeky as Dave and they had struck up a fast friendship.

We often got together to watch movies and play video games, but I had noticed that she had started to come over and spend time with Dave, in his room, (which was located on the ground floor in our shared accommodation terraced house) when her partner was in lectures.

Most of the time the door was open, and I or my housemates would be in the lounge and could see that they were playing computer games or watching a movie or TV show.

It seemed innocent, but I mentioned it to my housemate who was part of the same social circle and she said it was perfectly normal and I was being paranoid.

This was my first experience of friend enablers. Of course, now I know that it is not normal to spend time with a girl in your bedroom, separate from the rest of the house when there is a perfectly good lounge in the room next door. But my "friend's" assurance that it was ok made me think I was being jealous or unreasonable.

I felt reassured that he was still into me when that year for Valentine's Day he bought tickets to see Reel Big Fish, and booked a hotel for the night.

I was delighted, the band played "our song" and I was looking forward to a romantic evening.

I was surprised when his best friend turned up at the hotel, meeting us in the lobby. Dave told me that I had *assumed* it was for Valentine's Day, that he'd never mentioned it (he had) that it was selfish of me to not want his friend to share the experience when it was one of his favourite bands, and that if I was going to behave like that he wasn't sure he wanted me to come.

The reaction to my comment that I thought this was our Valentine's Day treat left me feeling off kilter, and wondering what I had done. I must have done something REALLY BAD, despite the fact that I hadn't been being argumentative or trying to stir up trouble, I had just wanted to clarify.

The next big slip up was in front of my mum. He always worked hard to impress her and was the perfect gentleman. I was still so caught up in his spell and by this point, thought so little of my own self worth that I fully believed the impression he gave her, thinking that those "little incidents" were always because I wasn't good enough, I had failed him in some way, I wasn't intelligent enough.

This time though, he didn't lose his temper with me, or with my lecturer. This time he lost it with my Mum.

I'd always been very careful to not tell her about all the little digs and the bad moods or the manipulation, mainly because I felt it was my own doing, but also because I felt that he would be "misunderstood", and because I thought I was happy and didn't want her to think I wasn't.

So she was shocked by the person she saw when he lost his temper with her. She hadn't done anything wrong – she'd simply misunderstood a computer related discussion with him.

This was coming towards the end of our relationship and looking back he was at this point having an affair with our friend – so perhaps keeping up appearances with my mother was no longer a priority.

Six months before we broke up I finally managed to persuade him to rent our own house together. It was slightly further away from the student area of Leicester, but not as far as I would like. I had become more and more depressed, and was not getting any emotional support, either from him or from "our" friends.

My own friendship circle had long since grown sick of me never going to their parties or meet ups and drifted away – I do not blame them for this, a healthy relationship needs attention from both sides whether it is a friendship or a romantic relationship – and my hands had been full trying to juggle all of Dave's needs and wants and I had not had the capacity to pay attention to them too, something I am sure he did on purpose.

I stopped going to the Society meetings.

While my depression put the final nail in the coffin for it, I'd grown out of it sometime previously anyway and had only been attending in order to keep the peace with Dave.

Dave continued going, despite my asking him to stay with me occasionally on a Friday Night instead, maybe going for a night out or to the cinema. As I got more depressed, the less I wanted to leave the house at all.

More worryingly, Dave was spending more and more time with the girl from the other couple.

Eventually I decided to confront him about this. I assumed that he was innocent, that he didn't realise that while on his side he may feel only friendship, she definitely felt more.

There was precedent for him making this mistake, from when we had first got together. Or that's how it had looked to me.

The night I confronted him about it I asked him to choose. They say you should never force someone to choose between you and their friends. Of course – that wasn't quite what I was doing, but the effect was the same.

And it was THE BEST THING I HAVE EVER DONE IN MY LIFE.

Of course he did not choose me. I told him that I thought Sammie (not her real name) had a crush on him. I explained all the signals I had picked up on, all the little symptoms that showed that something was wrong.

In response, he called me a "psycho bitch" He told me I'd had problems with jealousy for a long time, although I had never mentioned it to him before. He told me that he couldn't cope with my selfishness and my depression. He told me that my depression was contagious and that he couldn't be near me any longer as it was making him feel depressed.

He said he would never pick me over his friends, and that we were over.

And like that, my entire life crumbled under my feet and I was freefalling.

I don't know how many weeks it took before I surfaced and was able to take my first deep breath of air. I know that when I did I had no friends. I'd lost my lovely house. I had nothing and no one. Somehow I'd managed to get a tiny little flat, mere meters from the lovely home I'd dreamed of being our first proper home together.

In December, around two months after the break-up, and just after Christmas – the 28th to be precise, I was sat alone in my flat scrolling through Facebook when I saw a post from a guy who had gone to college with one of the "friends" I had lost during the break up.

He had posted that he was going out, and if anyone wanted to join him then he would be at the Dover in Leicester. I'd only met the guy once, but on a whim I responded that yes, I would go out with him.

The moment I arrived at the bar he bought me a sambuca, completely ignored my refusals as sambuca makes me hurl, and insisted that I do the shots with him and another friend of his. I still wasn't out of the habit of "not rocking the boat" so I did the shots.

Alcohol is said to make people forget what they did the night they were drinking. But I remember every second of that night.

I remember laughing. I remember feeling happy for the first time in years. I remember going back to my flat and putting Florence and the Machine on and Ben singing along SO BADLY, and my not knowing what to do or how to tell him, and I remember thinking, well fuck it, if he's enjoying himself, what does it matter?

I remember us dancing, and I remember Ben falling asleep on my floor on the new rug my mum had bought me to try and make the flat a bit more cosy.

That night was the night that began my recovery. Ben quite literally pulled me kicking and screaming out of the pit that Dave had designated for me and taught me to have fun again, simply because Ben had decided we were going to have fun.

And the fun didn't end with that one night.

We built a cat made of snow on the path in front of my flat.

We met and befriended the girls that lived in the house next door and we went out with them, a neighbourhood cat decided he lived in my flat too and used to let himself in for snuggles.

We danced in my tiny living room and we laughed and we sang. We cried at stupid movies and we watched the sunrise out of my living room window.

Every day was busy, full of fun and I started to value myself more.

I realised that I was right to trust my judgement when I heard that Sammie and Dave had been caught in the act by her boyfriend, but I didn't care as much as I would have. I didn't care as much as I felt I SHOULD have.

I kept being nosey and investigating what they were doing, but it was just that – nosiness, rather than hurt and animosity.

I started dating again.

Not seriously - I was writing a blog and thought it would be hilarious to go on as many bad internet dates as I could to get experiences to write about. I managed to go on some fantastically bad dates.

They were absolutely hilarious, from the guy who reckoned he was mates with Florence Welch to the guy who honestly thought he was god's gift to women (I gave up counting how many times he checked his appearance in the reflection of the restaurant's window)

And then one of the dates was worse than all the others. It was a truly, truly terrible date. But this one was different. The reason this one was so much more terrible was because I actually cared about this guy. And I managed to arrange the most horrendous date I've ever done.

I accidentally took a guy who likes rock music to a VERY bad House/Jungle/Drum and Bass night, where we were the only people in the (rock) venue. I don't know why they chose that night to be the one night where they didn't play Rock music, but there you go.

Through some miracle he wrote the first date off, we've now been together for nearly eight years. Eight years of laughing every time we think about that bloody awful first date.

We have three cats. We're engaged. We own our own house

Everything I had dreamed and hoped and worked for in my life has happened, is happening, or will happen.

Phil goes out of his way to ensure that we reach those milestones. And now I understand, finally, that this is what a true relationship is supposed to be. Two people, working together to ensure that each other's ambitions come to fruition, so that when we get to the end of our lives we can look back and say, "We did that, together".

Happy Ever After

By Lindzi Mayann

Dedicated to my favourite King.

Happy Ever After, Happy Ever After,
Once Upon A Time she believed in a grafter.
Worked hard, loved hard,
Believed in happy laughter.

Happy Ever After, Happy Ever After,
Once upon a time, he said he'd never shaft 'er,
Played hard, strayed far,
Shattered ever after.

So the Princess kissed her frog and he became a Prince.
But where in the tale does it say he leaves her since?

That he'd outgrow the pond and become a star.
That females would cry his name from Kingdoms afar.

The Princess watched him go, she didn't bother to cast a
spell.
Instead she vowed she would always wish him well.

And other castles the Prince would go on to master.
Fair women visiting him, thicker and faster.

Of course it was inevitable, the Prince became a King.
And the Princess, still single, didn't let it sting.

And the next thing her King, was to be served.
An heir to his thrown, it was what he deserved.

The Princess was happy, the King must be happy, she felt sure.
He'd got everything he had dreamed of and probably much more.

But every King has his day and when his finally came.
He felt sure his wild ways were ultimately to blame.

The Princess was there for him, she would shield him from   pain.
She wouldn't hold it against him that she hadn't shared in his reign.

Now everyone knows fairy tales don't really exist.
But the King would seek her out and they would share a kiss.

And when their lips meet for this wonderful snog.
Oops, the Princess turned him back into a frog.

Mr. Hedgehog

By Alex Hall-Smith

"There he is, look." Said Alex, pointing out a hedgehog slowly making his way across the concrete path outside his ground floor flat.

"Oh yeah." Replied his girlfriend with the same amount of enthusiasm she started to display recently.

"Hello Mr. Hedgehog, been hogging many hedges today?"

"Huh." Responded his girlfriend.

"Did you get that? Because he's a hedgehog." There was an uninterested pause. "What I've done there is swap his name around and suggested that he's 'hogging' hedges."

Alex waited a long time for a response that didn't come.

"I have to go home." She said eventually before picking up her coat and making a hasty exit.

"Bye then." Tried Alex.

No reply.

Mr. Hedgehog had made his first appearance almost five months before, scuttling in front of Alex's flat window and climbing onto a grassy patch and under the shrubbery to the left.

Alex had laughed at how long his legs were and his girlfriend had enjoyed the spectacle as well. You rarely saw hedgehogs pottering around, at least, alive ones.

They'd seen Mr. Hedgehog numerous times over the coming weeks, he didn't come every day, but when he did Alex felt a surge of excitement, not in a sexual way, just ordinary excitement.

His girlfriend had shown it too, only after a few weeks she starting to become less and less interested, as if the mere sight of Mr. Hedgehog bored her.

It seemed that today had been the last straw, that Alex's insistence of waiting by the window at the same time everyday had been too much.

Alex picked up his phone to call but there was already a message awaiting him.

'I can't do this anymore, I'm sorry. Don't contact me.'

Alex reread the text and thought about replying. But what was the point? There clearly wasn't room in the relationship for the three of them, Mr. Hedgehog was more important to him than she ever was. With that, he deleted her number and went back to the window. Mr. Hedgehog was long gone and Alex let out a sigh.

"Oh Mr. Hedgehog, do come back tomorrow."

Alex's hastily made 'Missing' signs adorned the streets for a mile in every direction from his front door.

Lampposts, bus shelters and anything with a space were used. The posters were simple, a picture of a hedgehog, easily found online, and the words 'Missing Hedgehog, reward offered for any information, and Alex's phone number underneath.

It had been a month since Mr. Hedgehogs last visit to the flat and there had been no sight of him since.

After the first few days Alex had taken to walking around the flats that he lived in to see if he could find Mr. Hedgehog, but nothing. After a week he'd extended his search to the nearby park and after two weeks he'd started to forage through bushes.

The signs were his last resort and offering a reward seemed like a good idea. After attaching the last of his two hundred copies to a phone box, Alex made his way home to await the calls of good news he so desperately wanted.

Phone fully charged and a seat by the window was all he needed, now to play the waiting game.

Two days later the phone rang. Alex had barely moved opting for running to the toilet and refusing to shower or brush his teeth. After the first day he'd surrounded himself with food and water so that if Mr. Hedgehog had decided to make a welcome return, he wouldn't miss it.

The number was alien to him so he assumed it must be someone with good news.

"Hello?" he said a little to excitedly.

"Erm...Hello?" came the reply. "Are you the bloke looking for the hedgehog?"

"Mr. Hedgehog? Yes, that's me." Replied Alex, slightly annoyed at the fact he'd just said 'hedgehog' when the posters clearly stated 'Mr. Hedgehog.'

"There's a dead one outside my house."

Alex went silent. A knot had instantly formed in his stomach and he could feel tears begin to form. "Where?"

"You what pal?"

"Where did you see him?" choked Alex.

"Portland Street pal." Came the response.

Alex searched his brain. Portland Street? Where the hell was Portland Street?

"You still there pal?" asked the caller.

"Yes...yes, sorry." Started Alex. "Where's Portland Street?"

"Grimsby."

"*Grimsby?*" Choked Alex. "But I live in Leicester!"

"Oh right, probably not the one you're looking for then pal?" said the caller. Alex could hear that his voice had taken an amused tone; this was clearly a prank call.

"You think this is funny do you? Calling up and...hold on a minute, how'd you get this number?"

"Poster pal." Came the reply.

Alex thought for a second. How could this guy have seen his posters if he was all the way in Grimsby? That was miles away.

"How did you see the poster?" he asked.

"All over social media pal, fucking hilarious you sad twat!" With that the caller burst into laughter and hung up the phone.

Alex's tears began to fall and for a second he placed his head in his hands. That was until he realised he'd kept his eyes away from the window since the call had came. He quickly looked up, nothing, again he cried.

The mocking phone calls continued for the rest of the day and late into the night. Some were hurtful, others were just people laughing down the phone and a few of them were threatening.

"Bet that hedgehog ran off cause you kept trying to fuck it you wanker! If I see you around I'm going to break your fucking neck." Was a particular low point.

After three more days of abuse Alex decided it was probably best to leave the house and turn the phone off. He'd decided that he would try and look one last time for Mr. Hedgehog and if he couldn't find him, would have to try and move on.

He started with the bushes close to his front door, awkwardly making his way through the underground looking for clues. Luckily he'd found his trusty magnifying glass that made him look like a proper sleuth.

Nothing was to be found though so he continued his search around the bushes and trees around the flats.

When that came to nothing he searched the bins, underneath the cars and eventually, though he didn't want to, the road.

After hours of searching he finally decided to call it a day. The light was fading and other than get a torch, there seemed to be little point in continuing. Reluctantly Alex returned home and flopped onto the sofa. After a few moments he turned his phone back on to reveal fourteen new voicemail messages.

He knew he shouldn't listen to them as they would only make his mood worse but something made him.

The first five were the usual laughter and obscene language and referring to him indulging in bestiality. But what was this? There seemed to be a familiar voice saying his name. Of course, it was his ex-girlfriend. Maybe she would have some kind words of encouragement. Unfortunately while thinking about everything she might say, he'd completely missed the message and had to start over.

"Hi Alex. I've seen your posters and the social media stuff. Must be a really tough time for you, people really seem to have taken a disliking to you. You've even been ridiculed on the TV panel shows and no one deserves that."

The TV panel shows? Had it really reached that level?

"I'm so sorry Alex, I didn't mean for it to get to this." She continued.

What did she mean? What had she done?

There was a pause where she searched for the right words to say.

"Alex...I took Mr. Hedgehog. I was so angry with you for paying more attention to him than me I just saw red."

Alex felt the rage inside begin to rise.

"Don't worry though, he's safe. I've kept him in a box in the garden and feeding him, he's even put on a little weight."

That softened Alex a little and his eyes filled with tears.

"Listen, I'll bring him over tomorrow morning and we can talk. I'm sorry, I'll see you in the morning."
With that the line went dead and the phone moved on to the next message.

"You fucking cu.." Alex quickly ended the message and stared out of the window. He was okay, Mr. Hedgehog was alive and well and coming home tomorrow.
Sure he was angry at what had happened and what his ex-girlfriend had done but it was all outweighed with the prospect of seeing his best friend again, Mr. Hedgehog.

Obviously Alex had barely slept a wink that night and was up and sat by the window awaiting Mr. Hedgehog's triumphant return.
It wasn't until half past ten that he eventually spotted his ex walking down the pavement towards his front door, cardboard box in hand. Alex was too excited to wait and quickly made his way to the front door, flinging it open in excitement.

"Alex…" she started. But Alex cut her off.

"Please, I don't want to argue. You had your reasons and I'm sorry, but he's home now and that's all that matters."

She placed the box on the grass outside his house and opened the lid.

"There he is." Said Alex beginning to feel the tears coming again. He looked healthy and his ex was right, he had put on a little weight.

"Pick him up, you'd be surprised how soft they are." Said his ex and suddenly Alex realised he'd never actually held a hedgehog before. He'd thought that they would be spikey and dangerous to handle but when he bent over to handle him he was overcome at how soft and cuddly he really was.

"My god, he's so soft." He gushed.

"I know." Smiled his ex.

"I just want to cuddle him." Alex held Mr. Hedgehog close and felt as though he wouldn't ever let him go.

"Careful Alex, he's only little."

But Alex wasn't listening; he'd pulled Mr. Hedgehog close to his chest and squeezed him tight until there was a crunch and a whimper followed by a warm liquid running down Alex's chest.

Alex had loved Mr. Hedgehog more than anything in his life.

He'd literally loved him to death.

My Narcissistic Manager

By Laura Anna

I was going through a really rough time around six years ago, my life was messed up. In fact I was in the middle of a mental breakdown. I had three young teens and my long term relationship with their dad was on the rocks.

I moved out of our beautiful home, without so much as a teaspoon to my name, into the most depressing, damp hovel you could imagine!

Working crap hours, in retail on a zero hour contract, I felt lower than a worm's willy!

Then this woman, let's call her Helen, just appeared! She'd just split up from her girlfriend, I knew her a bit, as I was friends with her ex. I can't remember how we bumped into each other then or this time but she became the friend I really needed... Really quick!

She blew that much smoke up my arse, she actually made me feel like I was worth something, which I hadn't felt in a very long time.

Then she offered me a job as a receptionist at her place. I was thrilled. I'd only ever done minimum wage, menial jobs before so this was an opportunity too good to miss.

At work she was brilliant.

She had so much faith in me. She wanted to train me to be her assistant, more hours, better wage.

I'd only been there a few weeks and was not entirely confident with the reception work I was doing, but I threw myself into it.

Maths is my nemesis but I tried, I even went to night classes in maths to improve. But it was so hard and all the time she was telling me how useless the rest of the team were and how much she was relying on me so that she could entrust work to me to enable her to have more time off.

I was determined to make her proud, despite my own reservations.

During this period, I'd moved out of the damp, insect infested house and into a newish build. I was relying on tax credits to help pay my rent. I invited Helen round to my new pad for drinks. She was annoyed because I was living in a better standard of house, arguably better than the one she actually owned and lived in.

I was pretty shocked at her attitude, it was so obvious she was only happy to be a friend to me if I was beneath her! It really upset me.

Her entire attitude changed towards me over night. Since I was doing the assistant job training, I was working five hours a week over the sixteen hours you could on tax credits. As a result I was financially four hundred pounds a month worse off! I went to the finance director, explained the situation, my kids and I were literally living on £5 frozen meal deals, I was in debt and facing quite extreme poverty. I requested my hours to be dropped back down to my original sixteen hours, my wage hadn't increased, so it was pretty straight forward.

After this, life at work became a nightmare. I was hauled into the office regularly to be reprimanded for the most ridiculous of things, tiny things like I hadn't put paper in the printer! Some things I could prove were not my errors but these were still held against me and the people who were actually responsible were never bought to task!

I noticed she'd never take responsibility for her own mistakes. She would literally highlight everyone else around her as being useless to her boss to make her own position more valuable.

She'd stamp her feet to get her own way, she'd blow her own trumpet that much it was sickening. Her life over powered and over shadowed everyone else's.

She'd NEVER let you finish a story about how well your kids are doing at school or something, without her turning the conversation round to her and her family. In fact so often she'd even change the subject completely.

She'd take credit for absolutely everything and throw daggers in the direction of anyone who shared even a glimpse of the limelight she sought for herself. She would also make child's play of making you look foolish, stupid, incompetent and idiotic in front of others.

She bumped up my workload so she could watch me struggle and she'd constantly slag me off to my colleagues. She came across as sweetness and light on the surface. She manipulated her words and the people around her so expertly, you genuinely couldn't see it unless you were on the receiving end of her negative attention.

Everyone thought the sun shone from her arse! Or so I thought.

It didn't occur to me that my colleagues were fully aware of her narcissistic behaviour but blew smoke up her arse to prevent her turning her attention to them!

She advertised for a new assistant, told me I was never employed as a receptionist and by rights shouldn't even have the job. She told me to not bother applying for the position as despite my situation changing again and asking for more hours, she said I didn't have the mental capacity (as she twirled her finger at her temple) to do the job!

With a new written notice in hand for having a day off and being accused of faking illness (that went against every employment reprimand law) I was ready to toss in the towel. But I was back with my kids dad, back at home and planning our wedding, I couldn't afford to leave.... Yes, yet again her bad attitude towards me stepped up a gear as my personal life improved!

Covid 19- Our workforce being small and being of an average age of 65, Helen, her assistant (and new bff) Jamie (female) and I were propping up the business. All of a sudden she was back to blowing smoke up MY arse. I was putting in voluntary hours to help keep reception running and getting important orders that had been placed before lockdown, out.

She arranged for my 40th lockdown Birthday to be a lot more special than it would've been and I genuinely started to question my own attitude. Thinking I had imagined so much and had been far too harsh on her! I let my guards down and let her in again!

Three of our receptionists decided to retire once we returned to work after the lockdown. Helen had made a lot of changes, not only because of the Covid rules, but because she could!

She changed so much of our admin it was no surprise the others, who weren't able to come in during lockdown, couldn't keep up!

She told me I'd be getting a pay rise and would become the new reception manager.

She then went on to advertise for just one new receptionist to replace all three of my colleagues.

Despite telling me I'd have a pay rise and a change in job title, she's taken on the responsibilities of our previous reception manager, sharing these with Jamie... Who's been given extra hours.

This as a result of me asking for a bit of flexibility with overtime if I need it, because she'd changed the diary so much I barely have any time to keep on top of the tasks I'm already responsible for.

Incidentally I'm the only person there that hasn't ever billed for extra time!

I've been kept out of the entire interviewing process, despite being the only receptionist and she's started the new "highly qualified, amazing" receptionist conveniently whilst I'm on holiday!

I don't have any animosities towards Jamie or the new receptionist, but I do feel very much alone. I'm dreading going back!

I'd like to say that there's a happy ending or a solution but there isn't. I'm on good pay, I don't drive and my job is local. I would have to work full time on minimum wage to cover my wages and travel expenses... I feel trapped.

I go into work every day smiling on the outside whilst dying on the inside. Pretending to like her and being nice to her to polish the shiny veneer that she's created is so draining! It is all such a shame because apart from her bullying tactics, on the surface she comes across so lovely, yet it's just an act.

I absolutely love my job too, our clients absolutely love me and despite what she tries to do to sabotage me, I know I'm good at my job. I just know that at some point in the future if I don't jump, I will be pushed and it'll be at the cost of my reputation!

Sleep and Control

By Helen Johnson

Sleep was used as a form of control especially after we bought a house together when the children were small. I normally slept nearest to the door to allow me to attend to a child.

The children were waking up and disturbing our, but mostly my, sleep a lot less all those years ago. Barry's new sleep pattern, I thought was a sick joke. I bore the disturbed sleep of having two children with patience and stoicism, I loved them so much and I knew they would grow out of it.

Barry started to wake at 5am for weeks at a time and then stop only to restart after a few months. He didn't have this problem in our old house. He would become restless and then go to the bathroom and sneak in and make just enough noise to wake me. He never admitted he had a problem. I resented this "new" disturbance of my sleep. I wasn't able to catch up during the day. I wanted to have my sleep at night so I could get on with my day's activities. I wandered around like a wraith, I looked pale, old and terrible and I didn't look after my appearance.

I used to fold the laundry on the dining table, opposite was a mirror. I couldn't believe how awful and defeated I looked, pale, old and wrinkled. Eventually I moved the mirror away, I looked ill, neglected and defeated. I did nothing extra for my own pleasure. I ate more and Barry and I fought about it. He blamed me for being too sensitive and criticised my inability to get back to sleep.

Barry would take naps for up to two hours, I told him the napping was affecting his nighttime sleep but he wouldn't listen. When he was travelling I got my sleep, but I had more to do because I was alone with the children. When he came home, I relaxed a bit knowing he was available to help and the disturbance would start again.

He resented putting the kids to bed. "Why is it always me," he would complain.

Finally after two wretched nights in a row, I took the kids to IKEA and I bought two separate mattresses and two separate duvets. I slept better then.

After a time, I started to wear earplugs every night and as I realise now I'm very adaptable, I trained myself to get back to sleep, being angry and resentful doesn't help you to sleep. I learned to let go and I regained my sleep.

Towards the end of our relationship, Barry would fall asleep while I was talking to him. I said, "You wouldn't do that in a meeting, but you do it to me."

He never answered that.

When the kids were in bed and I'd cooked, served and cleared away the dishes, Barry rarely helped, I stopped asking, it was a waste of time. I would come into the sitting room for relaxation and then even as early as 8:30pm he would be snoozing. We used to hang out in the past but it was clear he was no longer interested. I would try to get exciting films we could watch to keep him awake. I suggested playing cards or a board game or just chatting but he didn't want to do it.

He didn't want to be with me, he didn't love me. If we sat together on the sofa, he would just lean on me and get heavy and fall asleep, especially if it was something I wanted to share with him.

Just as I got comfortable for the evening's relaxation, he would announce, "I'm going to bed, but you can stay up."

Then I would have to go upstairs, brush my teeth, get my pyjamas on and then go back down. I would have to creep in later to bed, alone and neglected.

Eventually I stopped doing that and if it was 9pm, I'd go to bed too. Then he would say, this is too early, I'll wake up early. I'd say, just read and then within minutes he would be snoring.

Sometimes he did wake early but by this time I had adapted to his disturbances, I had my own duvet, my own mattress and earplugs, I was immune. I was no longer sleep deprived but I didn't like the separate duvets, we should have been a romantic couple cuddling together in our love.

I believed in love and our marriage but he did not.

My natural time to go to sleep was always about midnight, winding down from about 11pm. If you get the kids to bed and tidy the kitchen by 8:30 or 8:45 tops, that gives you a solid two hours or even more to study, relax, watch a film, do a hobby, have sex and read a book, phone a friend or even…gasp…go out and have a social life.

This was denied to me, Barry went out every Wednesday night with the car. I didn't have a night I could go out.

He got his Wednesday, I got nothing. Because of the travelling, I couldn't commit to an evening class and I found babysitters difficult to get hold of, expensive and inflexible. I couldn't get them to commit either.

Barry was really down on me learning Dutch which I did during the day, I had to work extra hard to make up for the time away from home. I was isolated, discouraged and sleep disturbed, it took huge effort to do that class at all.

He returned late on a Wednesday night, normally he would arrive just before midnight. I had adapted to the earlier sleeping time and he would disturb me coming home.

He managed to stay up late with the "lads" but not for me.

Notes On Narcissists.

By Morgana Everthorne.

Have you ever wondered why Eve chose the apple? Why she disobeyed YKW and obeyed the Snake?

I have a theory. She met the world's first narcissist. She went against her instincts and she paid for it, dearly.

Because, thinking about it, doesn't everyone do that when they meet a Narc for the first time? (Unknowingly it must be said.) But we all just carry on. Swept up in the moments of pure Heaven and Bliss, and enjoying the view from the pedestal we are thrust upon.

Without realising it. We sign up for possibly the worst "thrill" ride ever. And then the fun begins...

I met my first Narc in 2010, after being single for nearly a decade.

I'm an Empath unfortunately so I do tend to "feel" more than most.

He was GORGEOUS. Tall, Dark haired and had the fantastic Cockney accent I had always adored. I'll admit I was unsure at first, and I refused to respond to his voicemails and texts about how he was "sweet on me." etc.

Unfortunately, after two weeks relentless pursuit, I gave in.

Then it began,..

He'd picked up on the fact that I was lonely, that I sought company and affection. That my own self esteem was lower than a cesspit. And little did I know, he'd take full advantage.

The stories about his rough childhood, his mother kicking him out. Him being yanked in and out of care three or four times. Him living in squats for four years, for starters.

I should have known from the beginning, it was all about him.

But I was so blinded by what I thought was light, I couldn't see him dragging me into the darkness that surrounded him and would soon drag me in too.

At first, he ADORED me, he would say how happy I made him. That I was his saviour. I did everything for him.

I shopped, I cooked, I became his nurse, his counsellor. But it was never enough. As I soon found out. Those things he adored, soon became those things he hated. My devotion to family and friends soon became an inconvenience. Because the more time I devoted to them, the less I devoted to him. And I paid, dearly...

He soon distanced me from friends, coming up with excuses as to why I couldn't see them. (He told me that he had Hepatitis C from the beginning. He was also a Heroin addict. But more on that later.) he resented me working due to the fact I had Sciatica and two slipped discs. *Spoiler. It was because I wasn't his slave 24/7.*

I was punished if he didn't do what he wanted, verbally and physically. I was a bitch, a demon, a whore, a degenerate, among other things. I was dragged out of his front door in the middle of the night and forced to stand in my underwear (Usually at around 2am in freezing temperatures.), dragged from one room to the other if we had rowed. (Bruises to prove it)

He became paranoid about a new neighbour downstairs and became convinced he was robbing him and spying on him.

Left used needles in every place possible. (One got lodged in my spare pillow, resulting in an Emergency Trip to A and E. No remorse, whatsoever.) I spent an awful and undignified afternoon being tested for Hepatitis and Lord only knows what else, but thankfully these were all negative.

However, it took my Father's illness and untimely death for me to finally escape. After a rush into ICU, and over a week of intensive tests of every bodily fluid and function possible, we finally found out what had been ailing my Father so badly.

After an operation to drain fluid from his left lung (resulting in three litres of fluid and a nasty case of Cellulitis.) he was allowed home. His time with us there was brief. He was back in hospital within twenty-four hours, and there he resided on the chest and lung unit for nearly three months.

One truly awful morning, I received a phone call from my panicked Mother. He had been rushed to ICU as he was having trouble breathing, and I was told, "You should be here." No prizes for guessing what that meant...

For over a week, we waited, counting each day. Then on the 9th day, our worst fears were confirmed... Dad had ended up with Candida and E-Coli present in his lungs. (They had found it by scraping a miniscule amount of bacteria in his breathing tube. Having been put on a ventilator on his arrival in ICU.) They gave him a week to live; He lasted less than 48 hours.

On the 25/10/2016 at approximately 12:51pm my Father died of a massive Cardiac Arrest, with me holding one hand, and my Mother the other.

Now, you would think that a man who truly loved his partner of seven years would be sympathetic and supportive, yes? Not so. He hardly batted an eyelid when he was informed that my hero, my confidante and my best friend had died. I didn't see him for over three weeks, what with informing family, legal matters and trying to console my Mother who had lost her soul mate and husband of over forty years and arranging the funeral, his last hurrah.

The day passed in mostly a blur in some respects, Reading for him, and trying to make sure those that had attended his Funeral and Wake knew just how much it meant to us that they were there, to celebrate his life and his achievements rather than mourn his passing.

And celebrate we did, memories were shared, music was played. We ate, we drank. We gave him the knees up he'd have been proud of. He'd have been so touched at what he meant to people. He was a proud man. And didn't really see what others saw, more's the pity.

Unfortunately, that day was marred by that "thing," I called my partner in life at that point. The day before, I had specifically asked my Monster in Law to keep him calm, as I needed to be there for my family, and to grieve. She let me down... spectacularly.

She engineered a row and left that morning. Leaving him with no dinner... So spoilt was he, he couldn't handle this. Resulting in fifty-two calls and uncountable texts, because I ignored him. (LET ME GRIEVE, FFS.)

I finally gave in at 2am as I couldn't sleep. Too eaten up by sadness and desolation. And he let rip. I was selfish, a bitch, I put him above my Father, etc... Resulting in a further week's silence.

Then, when I visited him after that week, it all clicked in to place. His actions proved that.

I first got screamed at as I hadn't brought him cigarettes or any alcohol, I'd kept him waiting for the supposed "untraceable." phone he'd insisted upon as by that point he'd convinced himself he was being "tracked" by the Government and his neighbour was out to destroy him. (Hence why he wouldn't use the phone I'd gifted him. A mint condition Galaxy Note 3. My fault again for giving him and "Unsecured" phone) I ended it there and then.

He refused to let me leave, so I snapped.

I'm not proud of this, but I pulled a knife from the drawer, and threatened to cut his throat. He soon backed down and let me go. Then followed two more years of agro.

I may have been single in a way, but he loomed over me like a black cloud. Everything was my fault, I'd destroyed our relationship, he'd given me everything. (BS. No Christmas or Birthday presents in five years as he was too goddamn lazy to leave the house or think of anyone other than himself.)

But I did heal, and I did move on. My feelings for him were dead in the water, and I didn't want to be alone any more. So I joined a couple of dating sites. (BIG MISTAKE)

After the usual ream of idiots, liars and Married men sending D**k pics. (I saw more d**k in three months than I did in seven years.) I met my what can only be described as, "Nemesis."

On first appearance, he was marvelous.

Funny, kind, and we had SO many shared interests. Music being the main draw.

We had so much in common; we hated liars, cheats and Narcissists. God I was a bloody fool!

Unfortunately I was so blindsided by his charm and patter it didn't register at all at first.

The deep texts, video chats and four hour long phone calls late into the night had me hooked. I was in love with him long before I realised.

My opinions mattered, I mattered.

For the first time in nearly a bloody decade! I was entranced, hypnotised and I LOVED IT. For the first time in years, I felt special. I was a fly in his web of deceit, and I couldn't see it. At All.

You see, little did I know at that point, I was feeding him ammunition, the very things I thought would bring us closer together would eventually give him cause to drive us apart and almost end me and my sanity.

Our first date took place after my Mother's initial consultation for treatment for Brain Cancer, one of the many she had been diagnosed and assigned treatment for. He knew this, and he couldn't have been more understanding or caring had I wished for it upon a star, or cast a spell.

We met at a well known station, after a couple of panicked phone calls from both of us, each convinced one had stood the other up. He was charm personified, told me my pictures didn't do me justice. That he truly couldn't believe his luck. And truth be told, neither could I.

We talked and talked, as if we'd known each other forever.

He met friends, who told him he'd landed a good 'un and to look after me.

We danced, we drank, I spoke to his Mother. (Who seemed ecstatic he'd met someone like me.)

We discussed dreams, hopes, our deepest fears and what we wanted from life. We finally said goodbye at 2am. And I had truly never felt so happy, and dare I say it complete in all my life. I actually had a lump in my throat when we said goodbye.

I truly believed I had found happiness for the first time in my life. And from his words I believed he had too.

"I'm thinking about you non stop." "You've made me believe in love again." Goddesses, he was full of it. And I was sucked in. I believed every word. Idiot that I was.

I fell for him hook, line and sinker. Which is clearly what he wanted all along. As later events would prove.

The next few weeks can only be described as the stuff of dreams, I felt loved, appreciated and I fell even deeper in love than I could have ever imagined. We were inseparable, you couldn't slide a ruler between us.

He met my Mum, who possibly adored him more than I did. He met my friends, who were finally relieved to see me so unbelievably happy.

Everyone loved him and accepted him as a part of my life, a permanent fixture. And I truly felt that for once, I'd got it right.

Then it shook. He was virtually living with me and my Mum at this stage. His belongings were with us. He'd come home and have dinner, his laundry would be done. And we'd have nights in front of the TV and just be happy. No words were needed, and if they were, it was only to complete the other's sentences.

Yeah, ok he drank, but as I did myself I never paid much attention.

Then the late nights started, he'd got delayed at work, the trains were up the wall, he'd lost his Oyster, etc.

I swallowed it, because I loved him.

Then it kicked up a gear, he'd disappear for two or three days at a time. He'd had to work away, he'd broken his phone. Family were ill.

That's when a message from his ex received two weeks after we became a couple rang in my ears. She'd said he'd beaten her up, that he was a cheat a liar and a scumbag. I'd ignored it. Yet I began to question everything.

And again I ignored it. To my cost.

He'd always had "unusual" tastes, but I happily went along with things, as I wanted to keep him happy. No one had ever asked me about what I wanted before, so I assumed it was normal.

Then I began to think back. And I realised none of it was. I had been fooled from day one.

We had talked about past relationships, which I happily told him about as I didn't want there to be any secrets between us. He was divorced, his first wife lived abroad, and he hadn't seen his son in over a decade. His next girl-fiend (pun intended.) was a raging drug addict and violent. And the one after that, was also an addict, and a liar who was "obsessed" with him, (Do you see a pattern forming? Because I wish I hadn't been so blind and seen it also.)

In every story, he was the victim, including in why his family, apart from his dear Mother did not speak to him, Work was also thin on the ground as he was always saying he couldn't trust many people, usually because of an argument or disputes over money.

So here goes. I'll try and give you a breakdown dear reader of everything that happened,

As you know, everything was beyond perfect to start with, then the more sinister side of his nature began to appear.

The first time we slept together, he tried to put his hands round my throat. I stopped him. I have to admit I was a little freaked out. Not enough to walk away unfortunately. I did notice some bruising on my upper arms, but put that down to passion and the heat of the moment.

His temper would turn on a sixpence, once when he mentioned he was going grey. I tried to reassure him that it didn't matter, as I was too. He flipped, telling me to stop comparing myself to him, that I was vain and I had no idea about him. (That at least was true.)

He'd use bottles and other objects on me, he'd pounce on me and when I complained it hurt as I wasn't ready, he'd say I was. And carry on regardless while I bit my lip and whimpered into my pillow.

"Stop being such a baby." He'd say. Then finish up and sleep. While I stared at the ceiling, second guessing myself. Which would soon be my normal.

Yet I accepted this as I assumed all couples did this, I'd never really known any different, you see. These instances always would be followed by a charm offensive, apologies, presents etc. So I happily carried on and we made plans for our first Christmas together where he would meet everyone.

I was disgustingly happy, it must be said.

All was fine, we checked into a hotel near my sister, and prepared to celebrate with my mum, my sister and our extended new family which we had gained when my sister married.

We shopped that afternoon, giggling over jewellery in shop windows, then went out for dinner with my mum, my sister and her husband. Yet, when we got back, his mood changed abruptly. (I was on antibiotics for what I thought was a UTI, it turned out to be an STI instead, I later found out.) I didn't want to be touched.

I felt fragile and ill, I said.

He said I stank, that I was a filthy, rotten tramp, that he would rather walk home than spend Christmas with me. He then stormed out, leaving me a sobbing mess in the bath. While I scrubbed myself raw, anything to get him to take back those evil things.

I put on a clean nightie and waited.

I woke up to him looming over me. He apologised and went to kiss me. I couldn't, as I was still terrified and I turned my head away. What happened next has haunted me ever since. He forced me onto my front, and took me.

I'd said no, that I didn't want to. But he did anyway. I had the phrase, *"Don't be such a baby,"* ringing in my ears for days.

The next day, we had a beautiful Christmas, he played up to everyone, and I was still blissfully happy to be his. He'd conditioned me to think that way you see.

Over the next few weeks, he distanced. And I didn't know why. Yet strangely I could feel it was the beginning of the end. And that scared me even more. I loved him, I needed him. He couldn't leave me, but leave he did.

We were meant to go out one Friday, he said he was working and couldn't make it. I went anyway. Much to his chagrin.

Two days later after giving me the silent treatment, he messaged to say he needed a break. Which I let him have as I was so desperate to keep him.

A week later, he'd cut me out completely, and even his Mother who I got on with, wouldn't give me an answer.

I found out later, from my own research, he'd told her he'd finished with me. And he had a new girlfriend. And he also was a woman beater and bad news, from an anonymous family member.

In short, I'd had a lucky escape. You see, he'd been asked to leave his wife, by her family due to his horrendous temper. His ex, who was lucky to be alive after one of his tirades, had pressed charges. (Hence why she'd messaged me. Still terrified of him.) I wish I'd listened, but you don't when you're in love, do you?

His entire family had disowned him, and were too terrified to say why. And the dog he said he'd given away hadn't been. He'd lost his rag and kicked it to death. The poor little scrap. He was a monster, a degenerate, an a**ehole. A lucky escape indeed, yes?

It didn't seem that way. For months I woke up screaming, convinced he was still there. I haven't heard from him since. Nearly a year now. I hated myself for still loving someone that didn't ever love me back.

In closing, I am healing my battered heart and self esteem slowly, but it will be a while before I ever trust anyone again.

Perhaps one day I will...

Dawn of the Living Dead

By Gary Clarke

First time in recovery I met my baby mother.
At this time in life, needed no other.
Maybe I thought this was the way to recover,
Had our first son, Callum, then Jacob, his brother.
Always inside, maybe another.

An erratic relationship, from the start,
17 years later, woman broken apart.
Feels so worthless, heart snapped in half.
But trust me she will always have a part.

We split up, and she fucked off alone,
Left me with boys, I'd never had known.

She went downhill drowning her so called sorrows,
Not giving a fuck if she wakes up tomorrow,
The buzz and fake high she was to follow,
Not knowing her life was to become so hollow.

Lowering her standards, on corners selling herself,
So fucking vulnerable not accepting the help.
Crack cocaine, they're constantly in her head.
My nickname, 'Dawn, of the Living Dead'.
She always walks around at one hundred miles an hour,
Always protesting, I'll change my ways tomorrow.

But Dawn, if you're listening, tomorrow never comes,
Come on fix up, and add up your sums.
Dawn of the light, not Dawn of the dead,
I just hope one day crack leaves her instead.

The Other Woman

By Billie Loucan

When I first met him I was working as a tutor at my first college appointment, he was doing work in the construction department. I saw him and thought he looked cute, a bit younger than me but still he made me smile instantly.

Later that day, the construction tutor came in to me and gave me the guy's number. I was dying with giggles, I couldn't message him! So I gave him mine to give back.

We started messaging then before I knew it I was finding any excuse to go to the construction department just to see him. I found myself liking him, a lot. After a few weeks of messaging I found out he had a girlfriend. I was really bummed but thought fuck that, I'm not that kind of girl. I told him so when I next saw him and we left it there.

About a year later I got a random text, it was him, asking how I was and did I remember him? He told me that he had split up with his girlfriend. It was around the beginning of December and we had been messaging for about a week before he asked me if I wanted to go to Amsterdam for New Year's Eve with him.
Normally I would have said no but something about him made it seem so exciting so I thought fuck it why not and I said yes.

It was so impulsive, not like me at all. I was in a whirl all day. He came round to mine that night to book. It was the first time I'd seen him since we last spoke over a year ago. When I opened the door I couldn't believe he was stood there, looking not how he looked before. His hair was shorter, his face more mature, in fact he looked gorgeous.

I was definitely attracted instantly.

We had a great night, booked Amsterdam and had a few drinks to celebrate. Of course, he stayed over. Now, I'm not one to sleep with guys on the first night but technically I had known him for over a year and we had just booked a holiday so I thought fuck it...... well I was certainly glad I did. It was amazing.

We continued seeing each other up until Amsterdam and I couldn't wait. Dam was a great trip and we had an amazing time. When we got back I thought it might fizzle out, there was such a big age gap- eleven years!! But how wrong I could be.

We were soon spending all of our time together, he would ring me as soon as he got in from work to tell me he was home and that he would be round as soon as he was sorted.

He was great to be around, he made me laugh so much and he was so affectionate, he was like a magnet and I couldn't help be drawn to him and wanted to be around him all the time.

We went away again that summer to a log cabin for a week, he liked to fish and I was going to get pissed. We had such a great time. By this point it was around nine months in. I was so happy with how things were between us.

My friends had started to ask why we didn't do more couple things together, going out, hanging out with each other's friends. It didn't really bother me to be honest, as long as we were together. Why did we need to go out?

We never made it "official" on Facebook either. Again, I wasn't bothered but friends and family were asking 'what we were'. You know how it goes with labels. When I finally asked him why we'd never gone Facebook official- after all his profile stated 'single' and technically he wasn't. His response was a kind of brush off which hurt and made me realise deep down that I was bothered. Why didn't he want to take me out more? Or spend time with my friends? Or tell people we were together? What was wrong with me?

I put the doubts out of my mind. By the time Christmas came around we were still together. By now he was practically living at mine and things were good. I still loved being around him.

My birthday was in January and I was having a party, and obviously I thought he would be there. It was my birthday after all. Think again. He made some excuse. I was gutted but carried on and didn't let on to anyone how upset I was.

This then seemed to be how the next few months would play out. Him dropping me last minute, leaving me hanging then turning up late with about an hour before going bed or just not turning up at all.

He stopped being affectionate towards me making me feel like I had to beg for attention.

He started going away with his friends more and more, weekends here and there or sometimes by himself saying he just needed to get away for a few days. At first I had no reason not to trust him- if he wanted to go away with his mates I would never stop him.

His car which was his pride and joy, he was very materialistic like that obsessive even, all of a sudden was constantly out of action so I would have to go and pick him up.

I didn't mind it in a way, it was more time to spend with him on the journey. But even then he would be constantly changing the time to later and later making all sorts of excuses. I'd spend my evenings waiting for him to decide what he was doing.

My intuition started to kick in and I knew something dodgy was going on. Even his phone, all of a sudden was glued to his side.

It made me feel like shit. What was the point?

Whenever I would try to talk to him about it he would turn it on and win me round. He would be back to the guy I first met and I would think it must just be me.

I was completely unsure of myself. I didn't know what the truth was, I didn't know which of my own thoughts to listen to.

This cycle went on for a few months until the summer when I finally found the strength to end it with him.

He had just got back from Amsterdam and was supposed to be coming straight to mine. I knew what time his flight was getting in and the airport was only forty minutes away, and his mate was picking him up.

It got later and later and then the excuses started to roll in, his mate forgot, then his mate was on his way but ended up driving to the wrong airport- excuse, excuse, excuse. I said I would drive to his to get him when he finally got back. When he got in the car I said I couldn't be with him anymore, I said I wanted to be with somebody who wanted to be with me and make me feel worth something. I wanted a proper boyfriend.

He said that wasn't him and that he wasn't "that guy" he didn't want to be a boyfriend.

I was gutted but so angry. I mean how had I just wasted nearly two years with someone who didn't want a relationship or to be somebody's boyfriend? What the fuck were we then?

There was a text convo about his belongings which had been left at mine, but they were soon forgotten and so it seemed our 'relationship'. I was hurt and angry and all that but I also felt some relief. I didn't realise what a weight he'd become on my mood, my whole life.

Almost two months had past when I got a message from him simply saying, "if some girl messages you just ignore it."

I thought, here we go.

Well, all day I waited but no message.

Then the next morning a message came through on Facebook from a woman basically accusing me of leaving my coat in the back of her boyfriend's car.

What the hell!?

I had barely opened my eyes. But I knew full well I had not left my coat in the back of *anyone's* car and certainly not a lad's. I clicked on her profile and there they were, this woman and my ex in a fucking relationship!!!

I couldn't believe it. I felt like I'd been kicked in the stomach. I messaged her back saying it wasn't my coat and told her who I was. It turned out she knew all about me and that they had been together for about nine months or so.

To make matters worse she lived about ten minutes down the road from me. (He was a contractor and worked in other people's homes- I knew which job it had been too.) I felt so stupid, all the times he was out or away with the lads he was with her. All the times he'd wanted picking up later and later, he'd been with her. I could now piece together all the times they had been together not to mention what she had told me about it all.

No wonder he hadn't wanted his car parked at my house- all the problems he had with it didn't make sense. His car would have stood out like a sore thumb. She didn't live far away, it would have been obvious because of where my house is.

Now it *all* made sense.

We didn't speak for over six months after that before he started trying to make contact, trying to add me on social media then blocking me and unblocking me. After about a week of this he finally messaged.

He absolutely poured his heart out, claiming he had made the worst mistake of his life, I'm the only woman for him, he had broken up with the other girl, he wanted to be in a relationship properly with me, he will never forgive himself for what he did to me blah blah, he totally bombarded me with messages.

I entertained it for a day or to, I mean I felt I was owed an apology and an explanation.

He asked to meet me, to which all my friends were dead against. I agreed to meet with him but for no other reason than to tell him all about himself and to leave me alone.

When I met him he looked like shit and again was begging me to take him back. It was really hard but I stood strong and wouldn't budge. After all, he had led a double life for nine months of us being together, how could I ever trust a word he said ever again?

He was so convincing when he told all those lies. He was still so sure of himself though claiming he knew the last time we spoke wouldn't be the last time and that he would see me again.

I couldn't wait to put him in his place and tell him this would be the last time.

As hard as it was I left him feeling really good and that it was for the best, me walking away. He messaged a few more times after that but soon got the hint I wasn't budging.

A month or so passed before he started up again, trying to entice me into conversation saying he was going through our old holiday photos and listening to our songs. Again I made it clear I didn't want any part of it.

It was a Saturday night a few months later when I had a message request on social media from some woman. I didn't immediately open it as I thought it was a bit strange. My friend said it would be a sales pitch kind of thing and I put it out my mind.

A couple of hours later my phone pings and I knew by the sound of the alert it was another social media message. Before I could even reach for it, a barrage of other messages pinged through, I was a bit intrigued.

When I looked I couldn't believe who it was..... only the girl who he had cheated on me with claiming she had heard from his current, new girlfriend that *I* was back seeing him again as she had found my work badge at his house!!!

What the hell!!

She then sent me screen shots of pretty much identical messages he had been sending to me, begging her to take him back and that there was nobody else for him. The cheek of her, after gloating she was the other woman, she was now telling me what a prick he was and how she would never give him another chance.

Well, good, I'm glad! I didn't need all this convincing and yet the evidence just keeps on coming!

I then opened the message from the mystery woman and it was indeed the current, new girlfriend- although she was being far more polite than the other one had been. I replied asking about the badge, mostly because I panicked thinking a college ID badge might have slipped my attention. When could he have gotten hold of one, and me not have noticed! I also reassured her I hadn't been to his house in years by this point.

She then began asking all kinds of awkward questions about when I had been seeing him. I told her the dates we had been together- the kind of timeline of our 'romance'.

It turned out the girlfriend I was talking to was none other than the original girlfriend he was with when I first ever met him back at the college, when we had swapped numbers and been messaging. Poor girl.

She had been with him pretty much the whole time I'd known him which would have been around five years at that point.

Well to say I was shocked is an understatement!! How the hell did he manage to dupe all of us at the same time?? It also turned out the work badge was not mine. Same first name, different work so actually it turned out there was a definite fourth girl tucked away somewhere too. What a guy!!!!

When I reflect back I do still feel sad and angry and even to some extent still do question how could I have been so silly, but I also feel so free and happy now and like a genuine weight has been lifted. It makes me feel really proud of myself knowing that it was my inner strength that got me to this position.

Open Letter

By Anon

To anyone who has ghosted someone, or is thinking about it.

What you may not realise about the decision you have made, or about to make, is this: The poor individual more than likely has no idea that there is anything wrong. That your life together is perfect, that YOU are perfect.

The fact you've rebuilt their confidence, made them feel good. Inspired feelings that they never thought they could feel. Maybe it's a game to you, but to them, it means everything.

The fact you have built trust in them, in their families, which you will irrevocably destroy in a matter of seconds, will take time to rebuild. If ever at all.

The questions and the pain you leave behind. It's like mourning a death. But with no body to bury or grave to visit.

Please. If you have ever had a shred of human decency. End things properly. Not for yourself. But for them. Think of someone else, just once.

Me.

Turns Out I Was.

By DP

"Night babe, love you."
"No you don't, you're in love with the idea of me."
"No, I love you!"
"Mm"
...

"Have a good day at work darling, love you."
"No you don't."
"Yes I do!"
"Nah, you're in love with the idea of me."
"No, I love you!"
"Mm"
....

"Love you."
"No you don't, you think you do but it's only the Idea of me."
"Please stop saying that, I really love you."
"Mm"
....

"Love you babe."
"No you don't, you're in love with the idea of me."
"Mm"

Lindzi's Conclusion

Putting together this collection has been one mad journey- both professionally and personally.

I suppose the worst thing has been relating to far too many parts of all the stories! It's been painful, tear-jerking and wildly inspiring.

So, one big final thank you to everyone who shared their experiences and stories. And, to you readers for supporting the collection. Please share the word about our book and feel free to get in contact about sharing your own stories.

I think one thing we can perhaps all agree on is there are a lot of massive dick heads out there! And also many wonderful and cool people who, unfortunately, get taken advantage of. Plus those amazing humans who step up and support the healing journey.

I'm sure you'll notice your own themes to these stories too.

I realised being the 'target' of a narcissist is like a weird and back-handed compliment. If they want to latch on to you, destroy you, challenge you- whatever- they clearly think you're special and worth it. You match- if not exceed- their standards and expectations, you are 'as good' as they are! They want- possibly *need*- to break you down.

And as the old saying goes 'opposites attract'. If you're a natural empath you possibly attract more than a usual share of narcs.

Unfortunately, it seems if you're vulnerable then a narc will take advantage of that. So beware and keep an eye on your loved ones.

Don't let a narcissist use you as an extension of their own worth. Don't let them get to you, leave them behind, use your amazing and beautiful powers to create a life you're happy with.

Unless you're happy with that, of course. I spoke to three women, at least, who said they recognise their partner's narc traits but for varied reasons it works for them, for now.

I, however, do not believe in, 'Let him go and if he comes back he was always yours.'
Instead I now reckon, 'Let him go and if he comes back nobody else wants him- Let him go again!'

Narcissists- and fuck boys- don't leave you for somebody 'better', they leave you for someone who puts up with their bullshit.

I've had my fair share of narcissistic female managers too. They taught me a lot, so cheers to that.

Stay up-to-date on new releases by following my social media accounts (Lindzi Mayann: Facebook, Instagram, Twitter and also check out www.lindzi.co.uk for my blog)

I have so many more exciting and unusual projects in the pipeline including the launch of Gary Clarke's (original work featured) full poetry collection!

A new book is being written as well as a poetry collection of my own, so stay tuned.

Being the victim of any kind of manipulation is powerfully destructive. Please think about how any negative comments might affect those behind this collection. Turn the page for advice and options.

Advice For You

From You

Quickest way to get rid of a narcissist? Cut off the source of energy. Allow them to move on and find it elsewhere.

Those things that piss you off at the very start of a relationship will be the big things in the long run. Are you ok with that?

If he's older than 25, his frontal lobe is fully formed and he ain't changing his ways.

If they promise to change and after 2 weeks they're back to old habits, forget it, walk away.

It. Doesn't. Get. Better.

If you mention your concerns to them and they call you a 'psycho' there is something wrong.

Trust your intuition and instincts- always.

No one reacts more dramatic than someone that definitely did what they're being accused of.

Joke's on you. You didn't break me. You lost the best thing you'll never have. You will never know true love, true happiness or true friendship. And I pity you.

No one changes unless they want to. Not if you beg them. Not if you shame them. Not if you use reason, emotion, or tough love. There's only one thing that makes someone change; their own realisation that they need to do it.

Being nice literally gets you nowhere unless you want to be a full time doormat.

Their heart is so large that they don't even know how to give up on people, even when they don't deserve it.

Repeat this until you understand it: I do not need people who do not need me.

Sometimes you have to make a decision that will break your heart but give peace to your soul.

I once loved someone so much that I was fixing them while they were breaking me.

You will never get the truth out of a narcissist. The closest you will ever come is a story that either makes them the victim of the hero, but never the villain.

Q: What have a serial-abuser and a leopard got in common?
A: The leopard can't change his spots and the abuser can't change their ways.

If you have to change into something that you don't want to be to please someone else then they aren't worth your time.

No one can throw a bigger tantrum than a narcissist who is losing control of someone else's mind.

Stop breaking yourself down into bite sized pieces to serve others. Stay whole and let them choke.

Be careful what you tolerate, you are teaching people how to treat you.

Wounded people are dangerous. We always get back up.

You can't build with someone who ain't trying to help you carry the bricks.

Sometimes there is a person in your life who is an exception to all your rules no matter what they do.

Someone once told me not to bite off more than I can chew. I said I'd rather choke on greatness than nibble on mediocrity.

Having good support helps. Turn to what is available, family and friends. Surround yourself with strong minds and work on your own strength.

Support Services

I took to social media and gathered this list of support options from people who recommended them and/ or have used them before. I hope they are useful.

Contact your local council for advice. They should be able to provide you with a list of things available in your area and also support with issues such as changing the locks.

Refuge- Free phone 24-Hour National Domestic Abuse Helpline: 0808 2000 247 www.refuge.org.uk

Unwomen- www.unwomen.org/en/about-us/contact-us

Women's Aid- www.womensaid.org.uk

Mankind- Male Victims of Domestic Abuse- For Confidential Help, Please Call: 01823 334244 www.mankind.org.uk/

Citizen's Advice- Advice line (England): 0800 144 8848. Visit the website to chat online and find contact details for your local Citizen's Advice. ww.citizensadvice.org.uk

NHS- Visit this site and click services near you. Under the mental health section there is a list of relevant services. www.nhs.uk/service-search/mental-health

Relate- Relationship support for everyone www.relate.org.uk

UAVA- United Against Violence and Abuse www.uava.org.uk/contact/

Savera- Focuses on shining a light on subject's surrounding 'honour'-based violence. www.saverauk.co.uk/contact-us/

Maya Centre- a safe space run by women for women. Provides free counseling for women who have had traumatic experiences. www.mayacentre.org.uk/

Wish- UK-wide, user-led charity focusing on women's mental health needs and supporting women in prison. www.womenatwish.org.uk/contact/

Muslim Women's Network UK- giving Muslim women a voice in modern Britain. www.mwnuk.co.uk/

Women and Girl's Network- www.wgn.org.uk/contact-us

Imkaan- addresses violence specifically affecting black and minority www.imkaan.org.uk/

Leicestershire and Surrounding

New Dawn New Day- supporting a brighter future for women.
www.ndnd.org.uk/

Living Without Abuse- Help and support for anyone suffering   abuse
www.lwa.org.uk/

Let's Talk Wellbeing (NHS)-

Leicestershire:
https://www.leicestercityccg.nhs.uk/my-health/leicesters-health-priorities/mental-health/lets-talk-wellbeing-leicester-leicestershire-rutland/

Nottinghamshire:
www.nottinghamshirehealthcare.nhs.uk/letstalkwellbeing

Printed in Great Britain
by Amazon

56155396R00088